General editor: Graham

Brodie's Notes on Charlotte Brontë's

Jane Eyre

Graham Handley MA Ph.D.
Formerly Principal Lecturer and Head of English Department, All Saints College, Tottenham

MACMILLAN

First published by James Brodie Ltd
This revised edition first published 1986
by Pan Books Ltd

Published 1992 by
MACMILLAN PRESS LTD
Houndmills, Basingstoke, Hampshire RG21 6XS
and London
Companies and representatives
throughout the world

ISBN 0–333–58054–0

11 10   9   8   7   6   5   4
02 01 00 99 98 97 96 95

Printed in Great Britain by
Cox & Wyman Ltd, Reading, Berkshire

Contents

Page references in these Notes are to the Pan Classics edition of *Jane Eyre*, but references are also given to particular chapters, so that the Notes may be used with any edition of the book.

Preface

The intention throughout this study aid is to stimulate and guide, to encourage your involvement in the book, and to develop informed responses and a sure understanding of the main details.

Brodie's Notes provide a clear outline of the play or novel's plot, followed by act, scene, or chapter summaries and/or commentaries. These are designed to emphasize the most important literary and factual details. Poems, stories or non-fiction texts combine brief summary with critical commentary on individual aspects or common features of the genre being examined. Textual notes define what is difficult or obscure and emphasize literary qualities. Revision questions are set at appropriate points to test your ability to appreciate the prescribed book and to write accurately and relevantly about it.

In addition, each of these Notes includes a critical appreciation of the author's art. This covers such major elements as characterization, style, structure, setting and themes. Poems are examined technically – rhyme, rhythm, for instance. In fact, any important aspect of the prescribed work will be evaluated. The aim is to send you back to the text you are studying.

Each study aid concludes with a series of general questions which require a detailed knowledge of the book: some of these questions may invite comparison with other books, some will be suitable for coursework exercises, and some could be adapted to work you are doing on another book or books. Each study aid has been adapted to meet the needs of the current examination requirements. They provide a basic, individual and imaginative response to the work being studied, and it is hoped that they will stimulate you to acquire disciplined reading habits and critical fluency.

Graham Handley 1991

The author and her work

Charlotte Brontë was born on 21 April 1816 at Thornton in Bradford, where her father Patrick, who was of Irish extraction, was Rector. Her mother, who came from a Methodist family in Penzance, Cornwall, had met her future husband when she was staying in Leeds. Maria Branwell brought her husband an annuity of £50 when they were married in 1812. Charlotte was the couple's third child, Maria and Elizabeth being babies of two and one years old respectively when she was born. A brother, Patrick Branwell (but known by the latter name) and two more sisters, Emily and Anne, were to arrive in the next few years, Anne, the youngest, being born at the beginning of 1820.

Soon after Anne's birth, Mr Brontë and his family moved to Haworth near Keighley in Yorkshire, where he had just been appointed parson. When Mrs Gaskell came to write her celebrated *Life of Charlotte Brontë* (1857), one of the classic biographies, which is still in print, she provided many facts and incidents which define the bleakness of the country around Haworth. Yet she acknowledged how rough though 'powerful in mind and body' were the people who lived in the area. The parsonage was quite small, and both parsonage and church were below the level of the churchyard which lay on two sides of the garden. The situation was both depressing and unhealthy. It was subjected to the fierce winds and driving rain which were characteristic of the district, and exposure to them certainly helped to sow the seeds of illness in the Brontë children. Nevertheless from the outset they chose to walk on the moors that rose above the village and which, as time went on, they grew to love passionately.

In 1821 Mrs Brontë died, and the children, who were already 'grave and silent beyond their years', were thrown more and more upon their own devices. Their aunt Miss Branwell came from Penzance to look after them; she was a kind woman who was determined to do her duty by them, but she found the change from the relatively warm south to the cold and bleak north distasteful, and spent much of her time in her bedroom. Though the children respected her they seem to have had little warm affection for her. She taught the girls needlework and household management, at which Charlotte was to excel; The Revd Patrick Brontë was responsible for his children's lessons. He was an eccentric man, had his meals alone owing to digestive trouble, and his theories on education were prompted by a 'desire to make his children hardy and indifferent to the pleasures of eating and of dress'. His decision to send his elder daughters Maria and Elizabeth to Cowan Bridge School in 1824 had momentous results for Charlotte's later fictional career. As Mrs Gaskell, invited by Mr Brontë to write a biography of Charlotte, wrote:

Miss Brontë more than once said to me that she would not have written what she did of Lowood in *Jane Eyre* if she had thought the place would have been so immediately identified with Cowan Bridge, although there was not a word in her account of the institution but what was true at the time when she knew it.

Maria was far superior to any of her playfellows and companions, and yet, she had faults so annoying that she was in constant disgrace with her teachers and an object of merciless dislike to one of them, who is depicted as 'Miss Scatcherd' in *Jane Eyre*. I need hardly say that Helen Burns is as exact a transcript of Maria Brontë as Charlotte's wonderful power of reproducing character could give.

Life of Charlotte Brontë (1857)

After the deaths of Maria and Elizabeth in 1825, and the removal of Charlotte and Emily from the school, the children were more and more driven into the world of the imagination. They built their own land of make-believe, putting their fancies into words, the juvenilia existing today in a number of tiny books about two inches square in which their stories were written. The handwriting is so minute that it can hardly be read without a magnifying glass. In her *History of the Year 1829* Charlotte tells us how their plays originated:

I will sketch the origin of our plays more explicitly if I can. First *Young Men*. Papa bought Branwell some wooden soldiers at Leeds; when Papa came home it was night and we were in bed, so next morning Branwell came to our door with a box of soldiers. Emily and I jumped out of bed, and I snatched up one and exclaimed, 'This is the Duke of Wellington! This shall be the Duke!' When I had said this, Emily likewise took up one and said it should be hers; when Anne came down she said one would be hers.

Branwell describes how the twelve wooden soldiers (now become twelve young men) founded a kingdom in Africa called Great Glass Town, about which innumerable histories, newspapers, magazines were written by the children. When Charlotte went away to school in 1831 the four 'chief genii' who helped the twelve, Tallii (Charlotte), Brannii (Branwell), Emmii (Emily), and Annii (Anne) decided to destroy the Great Glass Town. Charlotte wrote a poem about this, but while she was away Emily and Anne invented another world of make-believe, this time called Gondal. When Charlotte returned, she and Branwell originated yet another kingdom, this one called Angria, which lay in the east of Glass Town and was conquered by two pitiless Dukes. Charlotte found this dream world a pleasant escape from the tedium of reality, but she was aware of the dangers of living too much in the imagination – 'it makes the dreamer feel society, as it is, wretchedly insipid' – and in 1839 she renounced the land of Angria.

Charlotte stayed at Roe Head school for 18 months, 'a plain, short-sighted, oddly-dressed, studious little girl', becoming friends with Ellen Nussey and Mary Taylor. The letters and descriptions of these two provided Mrs Gaskell with much material about Charlotte when she came to write her life of the novelist. On her return home Charlotte helped to educate her younger sisters until, in 1835, she returned to the school as a teacher, taking Emily with her. Later on Emily became so home-sick that she had to go back to Haworth and the same thing happened to Anne, who had replaced her.

Charlotte and Anne later obtained posts in private families, but both were unfortunate in their employers, and soon changed their positions. Meanwhile, Branwell, who had hoped to study painting at the Royal Academy School, was disappointed – he had obviously given himself up to some degree of dissipation – and tried job after job, losing each in turn. Charlotte wanted them all to open a school, but the competition was such that she felt perhaps it was best to study in Brussels for some time in order to equip herself better for this scheme. It was in 1842 that she and Emily became pupils at the *pensionnat* of Madame Héger. They worked hard there, but decided to return home when they learned that their Aunt Branwell had died. Emily elected to stay with her father, while Charlotte returned again to Brussels, this time in the capacity of pupil-teacher. Her Brussels life is to a certain extent mirrored in *Villette*, but she experienced much loneliness and depression. This was in part owing to homesickness – the holidays were a particularly bad period to get through – and in part owing to the fact that she had fallen in love with Monsieur Héger, Madame's husband, who was a professor at the boys' school next door. Charlotte returned home in 1844, and plans for their own school were again much in the sisters' minds.

This time a domestic crisis killed off their hopes; Branwell came home in disgrace and from that time until his death three years later he was a constant worry to his family. Charlotte's courage and integrity made her push on for herself and her sisters, and all three decided to try and publish their poems. The girls had to pay ten guineas each for the publication of their book *Poems by Currer, Ellis and Acton Bell (1846)* and a further £12 for advertising it, but their reward was to see it in print with the masculine pseudonyms they had adopted. It made little or no impact but it gave the sisters the spur to try and get their novels – for each of them had been working away at these – published.

In 1847 Emily's *Wuthering Heights* and Anne's *Agnes Grey* were accepted for publication, but Charlotte's *The Professor* was not; it is a great tribute to her stamina, application and imagination that she set to work on *Jane Eyre* despite the fact that her father had just had an operation for cataracts. When the novel was accepted it met with high praise from such discerning critics as Thackeray and Leigh Hunt, though *Wuthering Heights, Agnes Grey* and *The Tenant of Wildfell Hall* did not get favourable reviews. It was assumed by many that all the novels were written by the same person using several names. There was some suspicion of double-dealing, and accordingly Anne and Charlotte went to the offices of their publisher in London and convinced him of their integrity. Family sorrow, however, was near at hand. Branwell died on 24 September 1848 and a few weeks later Emily died too. Anne was already weakening. She died in May 1849, with Charlotte in attendance upon her.

Charlotte keenly felt the loss of her sisters but she returned to writing her next novel, *Shirley*. There was no one to talk to, no one to confide in, but she pressed on with this important novel. It is set in the latter part of the Napoleonic War and deals with the Luddite riots over machine-breaking, but it has the woman theme, which is virtually present in all Charlotte's books, in its determined assertion of the need for more positive occupations for women. *Shirley* was well received, and soon Charlotte began to pay the first of a series of visits to London. She met

Thackeray, to whom she dedicated the second edition of *Jane Eyre* (without perhaps realizing that Thackeray, like Rochester, had a mad wife who had once tried to commit suicide). Charlotte also became acquainted with her future biographer, Mrs Gaskell, herself a successful social novelist and the author of the superbly ironic and much-loved *Cranford*.

Charlotte's life and Haworth became more lonely and dreary. She thought she heard her sisters' voices and their cries, in much the same way as Jane hears Rochester's voice calling her name in the novel. Urged to write another book she complied, and the result was *Villette*. This was published in 1853 and is semi-autobiographical, Charlotte drawing upon her life in Brussels through the narrator, Lucy Snowe. The latter, like Jane, is poor and plain, but makes her way in the Belgian school and ultimately finds herself attracted to the unromantic and sarcastic professor, Paul Emmanuel. The ending is ambiguous, there is use of the Gothic elements and the supernatural, and a very vivid portrayal of Belgian life. Lucy is more complex than Jane and highly neurotic.

It seems likely that several suitors were interested in Charlotte, but in 1852 her father's curate Arthur Bell Nicholls proposed to her. Her father objected to the match, and, although Charlotte did not then find her suitor congenial, she later accepted him in 1854 when he returned to a neighbourhood parish. But her happy marriage lasted only a few months. On 31 March 1855 Charlotte died. Her father died six years later in 1861. He had asked Mrs Gaskell to undertake a biography of his talented daughter, and this was accordingly published in 1857; it ends with a fitting tribute from Charlotte's friend Mary Taylor. The words, I think, sum up the life and concerns of a great writer, and stand here as a mark of serious intention and rather sad commentary:

She thought much of her duty, and had loftier and clearer notions of it than most people and held fast to them with more success ... All her life was but labour and pain; and she never threw down the burden for the sake of present pleasure.

Literary terms used in these Notes

metaphor A comparison without the use of 'like' or 'as' – for example – 'I infused into the narrative far less of *gall and wormwood* than ordinary.' The phrase stands metaphorically for 'bitterness'.

simile A comparison which is formally introduced by 'like' or 'as' – for example – 'The kind whisper went to my heart like a dagger.' The comparison indicates how sharply, keenly, Jane Eyre feels the whisper.

irony Irony is the manner of writing in which what is meant is the reverse of what the words appear to say. Irony in *Jane Eyre*, often with a *satirical* intention, is fairly common; the author, or the narrator, may be laughing at or criticizing a character or characters. Witness the presentation of Mr Brocklehurst, or Blanche Ingram, where the *tone* of the author's presentation is ironic.

satire This is writing in which social affectations or follies in the individual or in society are mocked, the object being their correction. Lady Ingram and her group in *Jane Eyre* are exposed as social – and perhaps mercenary – snobs, but St John Rivers, for all his limitations, is presented seriously and without satirical commentary.

symbol A word or description which stands for something else, i.e. the stricken chestnut-tree which stands for the stricken Rochester both in his marriage and, later, in the fire.

Jane Eyre in its time

In a perceptive study published as far back as 1954 Kathleen Tillotson considered other novels of the years 1847–8 (like Dickens's *Dombey and Son* and Mrs Gaskell's *Mary Barton*, for example) in order to demonstrate their qualities. Charlotte was also in initial competition with Thackeray, for *Vanity Fair* completed publication in 1848, and for the first time Thackeray felt himself at the top of the tree with Dickens, in whose shadow he had long been. It was into this company, some ten years before the advent of George Eliot and before the prolific writer of the Barchester and Palliser series Anthony Trollope had made any mark at all, that Charlotte Brontë emerged as an important novelist. There is little doubt that she had studied the works of her great predecessors in the English novel. She admired Sir Walter Scott (1771–1832) who virtually established the historical novel, but did not like Jane Austen. This is not surprising, since Jane Austen's satirical and ironic accounts of civilized and refined society lack the action, the edge of violence, the dramatic characters of Charlotte's novels. Of her contemporaries, Dickens is the great social commentator, redressing wrongs by his superb propagandist virtuosity, his vitality, humour, tremendously zestful imagination, his inimitable style. His canvases are much fuller than Charlotte's, but he shares with her a sense of the macabre, of the sudden and unexpected incident, even of the supernatural, and certainly her psychological intensity – seen clearly and unforgettably in Jane Eyre and in Lucy Snowe.

There seems every reason to believe that while Charlotte admired Thackeray (in her dedication of *Jane Eyre* she calls him 'the first social regenerator of the day') he had little or no influence on her style. Thackeray is urbane, confiding, satirical, ironic, sometimes oblique, conversational, in fact a number of things – whereas Charlotte's narrative in *Jane Eyre* is tense with movement, incident, expectation, mystery. She seems to have been familiar with the Gothic novelists like Mrs Radcliffe, whose *The Mysteries of Udolpho*, published in the 1790s, enjoyed a tremendous vogue. The Gothic novels from Horace Walpole's *Castle of Otranto* onwards were often set in Gothic castles, with gloomy and morose villains and frightened and essentially chaste heroines; they had supernatural, sometimes vampire elements, mysterious happenings, strange and supposedly inexplicable manifestations. Charlotte appears to be adapting aspects of the Gothic mode when she sets up the mystery of Grace Poole and describes the lonely upper storey of the house and the fire. Further, Rochester's revealing of the creature to whom he is bound in unholy wedlock, and before that the wounding of his brother-in-law, plus such settings as the red room at Gateshead and Thornfield itself, all these are recognizably derived from the Gothic. What is different is that in *Jane Eyre* there is an emphasis on realism, on there being a logical explanation ultimately. In addition to this the characters – Bertha apart – are naturally motivated – making *Jane Eyre* a strongly individual novel in its time. Not for Charlotte, unlike Thackeray and Dickens, the leisurely unfolding over some 18 months of the serial novel with its sub-plot ramifications. In *Jane Eyre* there is what we might accurately call 'pace'. This is subtly varied throughout the novel, with high moments of dramatic expectation, as with the arrival of Rochester's house-party or, by way of contrast, Jane about to accept, under duress, St John Rivers's proposal, only to be 'saved' by hearing Rochester's voice calling her name.

The autobiographical mode (remember that the sub-title of *Jane Eyre* was 'An Autobiography') is sometimes though not that frequently used in Victorian fiction – the novel that springs to mind immediately being Dickens's *Bleak House* (1852), where just about half the narration is undertaken by Esther Summerson. Another aspect of Victorian narrative method is seen in Charlotte's use of the omniscient voice to address or influence the reader. The device is much employed by Thackeray in *Vanity Fair*, and by Dickens throughout his work; since *Jane Eyre* is written in the first person, however, it would be very easy to confuse Jane's voice with Charlotte's. 'Reader, I married him' is manifestly Jane, but the *tone*, particularly about the position of women, is very obviously Charlotte. And here she does break new ground in Victorian fiction. *Jane Eyre* is almost the first major novel where the role of the woman in life is seriously explored and questioned. Jane's stance from orphan to woman is marked by a positive independence of attitude, which can be best summarized by saying that women have the right to the same freedom to choose as men. Jane's story is a demonstration of individual courage, and indeed, arguably, Jane is the protagonist – she applies for a post at Thornfield and gets it, she leaves because she will not be a mistress later to be discarded, she makes her way with the Rivers family, she runs a school, she resists St John Rivers (who would have made her a spiritual/moral mistress), she gives Rochester life and ultimately rehabilitates him. The novel thus sheds new light on the idea of a woman being entirely responsible for herself, an idea which was certainly new in her day. Jane is the first heroine in the English novel who has the freedom of action of the modern woman and, like the modern woman, she has had to fight for it. *Jane Eyre* is an early example of what today we call feminism; Jane herself symbolizes the women who fight not for power but for the rights of equality, the right to choose, the right to let their own moral views have expression and influence. It is a startling assertion of independence in an age which still regarded women as subordinate to men. St John Rivers, in a sense, typifies a certain male attitude which has come to be called chauvinistic; Jane's resistance to him is the forecast of a wider emancipation to come.

Plot and settings

Plot

Jane Eyre is orphaned when very young and brought up by her widowed aunt Mrs Reed at Gateshead. Mrs Reed dislikes Jane and treats her very much as the poor relation, encouraging her three children to do the same. One afternoon when her cousin John has been particularly vicious to her, Jane, despite her physical inferiority, is goaded into retaliation and attacks him. For this she is locked in the red room where her uncle died; sensing his ghost there she becomes hysterically ill. Soon after this her aunt decides to send her away to school; Mr Brocklehurst, who is responsible for the administration of Lowood Institution, is told by Mrs Reed that Jane is a liar.

At first, in the severe winter, life at Lowood is very hard, but it is made more endurable for Jane by the kindness of the superintendent Miss Temple and also by her friendship with Helen Burns, who is already dying of consumption. With the arrival of spring there is a typhus epidemic at Lowood; Jane escapes the fever, but is grief-stricken when Helen Burns dies from her own malady. Jane continues for eight more years at Lowood and becomes a teacher there herself, but after the marriage of Miss Temple, Jane decides to leave Lowood. She advertises for a post as a governess, is engaged by a Mrs Fairfax of Thornfield Hall, and leaves for her new position.

Arrived at Thornfield Jane meets Mrs Fairfax, whom she learns is the housekeeper. One afternoon a few months later while out walking she is overtaken by a horse and rider. The latter has a fall, and Jane goes to help him. On her return to Thornfield later, she learns that the man is Mr Rochester, her employer. Jane settles down to the new routine (she already gets on well with her charge, Adèle), but she is puzzled by certain happenings, the first of which occurred shortly after her arrival. Meanwhile Rochester manifests great interest in her and in response to her integrity and independence begins to confide in her.

It is quite obvious that Jane is well on the way to being in love with Rochester and that he is somewhat fascinated by her unusual qualities. She soon has another opportunity to help him, for one night, woken by a strange laugh, she finds that Rochester's bed has been set on fire. She deluges him and the bed with water, and he acknowledges that she has saved his life. He asks her not to mention the fire, and leads her to believe that it was probably caused by the mysterious Grace Poole. Rochester meanwhile goes off to visit his neighbours, where he will meet the Honourable Blanche Ingram, a society beauty. Jane begins to think that she has misread his feelings for her, and looks at herself closely, stressing her own inferiority in terms of looks and status to the young beauty she has heard described. When Rochester returns with the house-party, chief among them the beautiful Blanche, Jane and Adèle observe them, and Blanche makes it clear that she despises governesses. Jane observes the charades, notes Rochester's attentions to Blanche and suspects that he will marry her.

Rochester spends one day supposedly away on business, and during that time Richard Mason arrives, as does a gipsy, who wishes to tell the fortunes of the ladies. 'She' does so, obviously disconcerts Blanche, and then analyses Jane's character, soon revealing that 'She' is Mr Rochester in disguise. That night Jane is woken up by Rochester, who wants her help because Richard Mason has been wounded, apparently by Grace Poole. Jane stays with him while Rochester gets a surgeon, and Mason is quickly removed from the house. Rochester confides in Jane that he intends to marry, hinting of course that Blanche Ingram will be his choice. Meanwhile Jane is called back to visit Mrs Reed, who wants to see her, as she is very ill. Arrived at Gateshead, Jane finds a sick and often mentally-wandering Mrs Reed, who tells her that three years previously Jane's uncle had written from Madeira. Jane reads the letter, in which her uncle stated that he was going to make her his heir, but Mrs Reed had told him that Jane had died in the typhus outbreak at Lowood.

After Mrs Reed's death Jane returns to Thornfield. She soon learns that Rochester has not married Blanche; he confesses his love for Jane and, tremulous with happiness, she agrees to marry him. Mrs Fairfax advises Jane to keep Rochester at a distance during their courtship, and this she does. As the wedding day approaches she feels increasingly apprehensive and, two nights before her wedding, she wakes to find a strange person by her bed. Her wedding-veil is torn in two. Rochester hurries Jane to the wedding, but the ceremony is interrupted by Richard Mason's solicitor, who asserts that Rochester has a wife. Rochester takes Jane to see his wife, accompanied by the solicitor, Mason, and the clergyman. She is locked up on the upper floor of the house, Grace Poole being to all effects her keeper. Rochester tells the story of his marriage, of the hereditary madness in Bertha Mason's family, and of its degrading manifestations in her. Despite Rochester's pleas, and with the opportunity of becoming his mistress, Jane, broken-hearted but typically not broken in spirit, leaves Thornfield.

She travels by coach for two days and arrives at a small place called Whitcross. She wanders about and, exhausted and nearly starving, she is saved by St John Rivers and his two sisters, Diana and Mary. They take her into the sisters' home and take care of her until she recovers, when St John gets her a post in a village school which is financially supported by a local heiress, Rosamond Oliver. The latter is in love with St John, who represses his own love for her because he is intent on being a missionary, and does not feel that she is a suitable helpmeet for him. After some time St John reveals to Jane that she has been left a fortune by her uncle in Madeira (he has succeeded in discovering her true name from a slip she made), and Jane discovers in return that her uncle was the Rivers's uncle. They are thus cousins, and Jane insists on sharing her fortune with them. This does not deter St John from following his original plan however. With the impending marriage of Rosamond Oliver to Mr Granby, St John asks Jane to learn Hindustani, to marry him and to accompany him to India. Dedicated himself, cold, unimpassioned, determined, his methods of persuasion are virtually those of moral and spiritual blackmail, but just as she feels herself succumbing Jane hears Rochester's voice calling her name. She sets off, and when she arrives at Thornfield Hall she finds that it has been burnt down in a fire started by the mad Bertha. The latter died in the fire but Rochester, trying to save her, was badly injured and lost his sight. He is living in seclusion at Ferndean, but Jane seeks him out, makes herself known to him, and marries him. Rochester gradually recovers his sight – he is able to see their first child – Diana and Mary get married, and St John writes to Jane regularly from India, though she knows that the last letter she has from him will indeed be *the* last, as he cheerfully welcomes death in the service of God.

Settings

The story is set in various identifiable parts of England, probably in the last years of the eighteenth and the early years of the nineteenth century, though historical chronology in *Jane Eyre* is unimportant; the fact is, as Jane Jack and Margaret Smith have indicated in the Clarendon edition of *Jane Eyre* (Oxford, 1969, Appendix I), the time-scheme within the narrative is precise and accurate to a degree. They calculate that Jane lived with Mrs Reed for ten years, and that the Gateshead episode as related in the novel occupies about ten weeks. Jane's early days at Lowood stretch to about four-and-a-half months; she stays at the school for eight years altogether, six as a pupil and two as a teacher. She is 'barely eighteen' when she advertises for a post, and a few weeks later she is at Thornfield. Three months afterwards she meets Rochester one afternoon in January, and the fire in his bedroom occurs in March. In April the house-party arrives, and on 1 May Jane sets out for Gateshead to visit the dying Mrs Reed. A month later she returns to Thornfield, Rochester proposes late in June, and the frustrated marriage is in July. Jane flees, spends August with her cousins the Rivers girls and St John, works at her school during the autumn, shares her legacy with her cousins before Christmas. We are well into the next year when St John proposes to Jane, having watched her 'for ten months', and at the end of May Jane hears Rochester's voice calling her. She leaves the next day (1 June), and a few days later she makes herself known to Rochester and their life together begins. Six months after this she first hears from St John Rivers, some two years after her marriage to Rochester his sight is partially restored, and later Jane refers to the ten years of their marriage. There are odd references in the text, like the one to Scott's *Marmion* (1808), but it is the inward sequence which is important.

The most easily identified location is Lowood, the description of the institution being taken from the Clergy Daughters' School at Cowan Bridge, near Tunstall in Lancashire. This school was opened in 1824, founded by The Revd Carus Wilson, and in that year the two elder Brontë children, Maria and Elizabeth, followed by Charlotte, were enrolled. Living conditions at the school are mirrored in the early chapters of *Jane Eyre*, with the outbreak of fever in 1825. None died, but the young Brontë children – except Charlotte – had already been ill and were in any case tuberculous. Maria came home in February, and died in May, while Elizabeth followed her, dying in June. It seems likely that Charlotte and Emily left the school in June, though Mrs Gaskell asserts the contrary. Charlotte was there for barely a year, and her account appears to be a strongly partisan one, for she believed that conditions at the school had contributed to the deaths of her sisters. She asserted that the Lowood section of the novel '*is true*', but her first biographer, Mrs Gaskell, wrote: 'I believe she herself would have been glad of an opportunity to correct the over-strong impression which was made upon the public mind by her vivid picture.' Mrs Gaskell's account of Cowan Bridge School in the biography of Charlotte also brought condemnation on her own head, since she had blamed The Revd Carus Wilson in no uncertain terms. In the third edition her views are somewhat softened, and she acknowledges that 'there were grand and fine qualities in Mr Wilson'. There have always been two views of The Revd Wilson, but there can hardly be two views of Mr Brocklehurst, who is modelled on him. Brocklehurst is given all Carus Wilson's Calvinistic severity and there are no softening qualities. Charlotte Brontë drew from life, and if her memory of what actually happened at the school contains some distortion (and this is by no means certain), it is nonetheless a blending of social and moral concern on the one hand and superb fiction on the other.

The other locations of *Jane Eyre* can be identified very easily; none is as significant as Lowood. The pupils at Lowood attend Brocklebridge Church, which is Tunstall, Cowan Bridge. It is three miles from the school, and the original of Brocklehurst, The Revd Carus Wilson, preached there, as does his fictional counterpart. The nearest town to Lowood School is Lowton, and this is certainly Kirkby Lonsdale.

Prior to attending Lowood Jane is at Mrs Reed's residence at Gateshead Hall. The original is Stonegappe, four miles from Skipton (itself only eight miles from the Brontë home at Haworth), where Charlotte was governess to the Sidgewicks from April until July 1839. After Lowood Jane goes to Thornfield Hall. This is six miles from Millcote (Leeds). Here there are probably two originals, the first being Rydings, the family home of Charlotte's great friend Ellen Nussey, which had among other things an oak split by lightning, one of the great symbolic features of Thornfield in *Jane Eyre*. The second is

Norton Conyers near Ripon, where the interior, with its oak panelling and portraits and a legend about a madwoman, all suggest that Charlotte, who had visited the place, incorporated them into the narrative of *Jane Eyre*. Near Thornfield is the village of Hay (Jane first meets Rochester in Hay Lane) which is Wath, Norton Conyers, while Millcote, six miles from Thornfield, is to be identified with Leeds. Mr Rochester's other residence is Ferndean Manor, perhaps drawn from the ruined house on the Haworth/Colne road at Wycoller.

Jane's third journey involves her travelling for about two days and ending up at Whitcross, which has been identified as Moscar Cross, about ten miles from Sheffield. The village where Jane finds shelter after all her travelling is Morton, readily identified with Hathersage (Derbyshire), again near Sheffield; while Moor House, Marsh End, which is the home of the Rivers family, is just a few miles from Morton, the original probably being Moorseats, near Hathersage. These are the principal locations of *Jane Eyre*, and one of the reasons for the strong sense of actuality conveyed is because the original existed and is revivified fictionally. Charlotte is the mistress of settings, so that we see the big schoolroom at Lowood and the black pillar of Brocklehurst dominating it as Jane fatefully drops the slate. The interior of the dreaded red room, the exterior of Thornfield, the garden where Jane walks with Rochester, her looking into Moor House, her contemplating the ruin of Thornfield which complements the physical ruin she is soon to see of her 'master', all these are 'settings' and each in its individual way testifies to Charlotte Brontë's narrative art.

Chapter summaries, critical commentaries, textual notes and revision questions

Chapter 1

The story, told in the first person, begins on a cold November afternoon. Jane Eyre has been orphaned and is living in the house of her aunt Mrs Reed, who dislikes her and resents intensely her living there. Mrs Reed's children John, Georgiana and Eliza are stronger than Jane physically, and are thoroughly spoilt; as the story opens Jane has been dismissed by her aunt for no good reason and has sought refuge on a window-seat behind the curtains in the breakfast-room. There she looks at the pictures in Bewick's *History of British Birds*, but she is forcibly interrupted by the bullying fourteen-year-old John Reed, who torments her and presently throws the book at her. Jane falls and cuts her head, and when John charges at her she is roused to desperate retaliation. As a result Mrs Reed is called by her daughters, and Jane is locked in 'the red room'.

Commentary

The opening of the novel is atmospheric, the day outside reflecting the inner mood of the narrator, who is picked upon by everybody. Already there is a mark of Jane's independence of character in her speaking up. Her study of Bewick shows her capacity for imaginative identification; there is a symbolic association in what she sees, for in effect Jane Eyre is like the rock which stands up in the sea. Jane is to stand up against adversity, the 'quiet solitary churchyard' perhaps has a prophetic association with the later death of Helen Burns, while the fiend and the horned thing represent Jane's childish fears. Already she has a love of stories, witness those she hears from Bessie, but reality contains more terror in the confrontation with John Reed. We note the deafness and blindness of Mrs Reed to her son's character, the humiliation of Jane as dependant, the un-Christian attitudes and, above all, the speed of the narrative and the physical action. The chapter ends on a note of apprehension after Jane's display of courage.

cavillers i.e. those having small, trivial objections.

moreen Strong embossed woollen material.

Bewick's *History of British Birds* Published between 1797 and 1804 with Bewick's celebrated wood-engravings to accompany the text.

letter-press i.e. the text.

Lindeness . . . Naze . . . North Cape The first two on the Skagerrak, south Norway, the third the most northerly point of Europe on the island of Mageröya, Norway.

'Where the Northern Ocean . . .' A quotation from 'Autumn' by James Thomson (1700–48) taken from his long poem *The Seasons* (1726–30).

Spitzbergen, Nova Zembla Groups of islands in the Arctic Ocean.

crimped i.e. using a hot iron to produce undulations in a material.

Pamela Novel by Samuel Richardson (1689–1761) written in the form of letters, and having a strong moral tone (1740).

Henry, Earl of Moreland The novel is by Henry Brooke (1703–83) and was published in 1766. It is better known as *The Fool of Quality*.

Madame Mope i.e. a derogatory name, since Jane is being accused of 'moping'.

over-application i.e. over-eating.

Goldsmith's *History of Rome* Oliver Goldsmith (1728–74), poet, playwright, novelist, essayist and historian; his *A Roman History* was published in 1769.

Nero, Caligula The first the infamous Roman Emperor whose cruelty made his reign notorious (AD 54–68), the second a Roman Emperor whose behaviour led to his murder (reigned AD 37–41).

Chapter 2

Bessie and Miss Abbot, the lady's-maid, eventually get the struggling Jane to the red room in which her uncle, her mother's brother, had died. The room is described – it is nine years since Mr Reed's death – and Jane looks in the mirror at her small and spirit-like self. She passes from anger to fear, her sense of injury making her first think back to Mr Reed; she is certain he would have treated her kindly. Then she sees a light on the wall, thinks that it may be the spirit of Mr Reed, and breaks down, desperately trying to get through the door. Though Bessie and Abbot come to her and she tells them of her fears, Mrs Reed arrives on the scene and, despite Jane's pleas, locks her in the red room again.

Commentary

Further evidence of Jane's capacity for resistance, with some insight too into the nature of servants, whose snobbery, particularly in the case of Abbot, is evident, though Bessie's is somewhat muted. The cruelty with which Jane is treated is deplorable, both at the beginning and the end of the scene, but before the end we are taken into her imagination and shown the sensitivity of the child. Jane responds to associations, here that of death, and its influence on her troubled and miserable present. The description of the room, detailed and chilly, contributes to the atmosphere of apprehension. In a strange sense the loneliness of the room mirrors the loneliness of its frightened inhabitant, and the use of the looking-glass has a dual effect – to show Jane herself as she is and to give her a spirit-like quality which sets her thinking of spirits, Mr Reed's in particular, and thus deepening her fears. Jane's sense of moral justice is apparent, her passionate nature shown in her avowal that 'my brain was in tumult, and all my heart in insurrection'. Jane is aware of her physical inferiority as well as her supposed social inferiority to the Reeds, but her imagination takes wing, again her sense of justice telling her that Mr Reed's spirit, its wishes violated, might appear to console her. Her imagination rules her head, she gives way, and we note the unprincipled cruelty of Mrs Reed.

Abigail Waiting maid, so named from the handmaid mentioned in 1 Samuel, xxv, 3–42.
Marseilles counterpane Coverlet made of a double cloth fabric giving a raised effect.
ottoman A low, padded, often armless, seat.
like a dark deposit in a turbid well Note the vivid image, typical of Charlotte Brontë's style.
opprobrium Ignominy, disgrace.
vassalage Servants, treated by Mrs Reed like feudal vassals.
an inviting bourne i.e. a destination or boundary, as in *Hamlet* III, 1, 79–80 'The undiscover'd country, from whose bourn/No traveller returns . . .'
I abhor artifice, particularly in children Note the irony of this – her own children are full of deception.

Chapter 3

When Jane wakes, she finds herself in her own bed, though it takes her some time to come out of her nightmare. Bessie is nearby, and Mr Lloyd the apothecary is in attendance upon Jane. When he and Bessie leave, Jane hears Bessie say that she has had a fit. The next day, Jane feeling somewhat better, Bessie brings her some food which she does not touch. However, she does want to read *Gulliver's Travels*, but finds that such is her state of mental depression that she can't respond to that either. Bessie doesn't help the mood by singing a ballad about 'a poor orphan child'. Mr Lloyd visits her again, and while Bessie is out of the room, finds out what did happen. It is obvious that he recommends that Jane be sent away to school; Jane herself knows from conversations between Abbot and Bessie that her father was a poor clergyman, that her mother was disinherited for marrying beneath herself, and that both her parents died in a typhus epidemic.

Commentary

Note the feeling of security and tenderness that Jane gains from Mr Lloyd simply because he does not belong to the Gateshead family. We also note the evidence of increased humanity in Bessie when she observes that 'Missis was rather too hard'. It is curious that Jane's 'fit' or nightmare should anticipate some of her later experiences – this shows Charlotte Brontë's sense of structure – with the reference 'Something passed her ... and vanished' and 'A great black dog', anticipating Bertha Mason and Rochester's Pilot. Jane's 'nerves' and her own tracing of them to the red room incident are evidence of the integrated psychology of character, and the mood occasioned by the punishment and its traumatic associations are seen quite simply in Jane's refusal of food and in her loss of delight in one of her greatest pleasures – *Gulliver's Travels*. Significantly she now finds Gulliver 'a most desolate wanderer', a phrase which fits Jane's state aptly. Bessie's song also mirrors Jane's state and looks forward to her later journey to Whitcross. Mr Lloyd's questioning of Jane shows him intent on finding out the truth, and it also reflects his humanity. Jane's independence of view is again stressed when she rejects the idea of joining any relatives who may be poor. School affords a means of escape. The upstairs–downstairs interaction is further stressed, with Bessie becoming softer-hearted, while the chapter closes on a note of irony with the two women discussing a Welsh rabbit – their ordinary appetites coming before any humanitarian or Christian feeling for Jane.

apothecary i.e. one who originally sold and prepared drugs, and here a kind of general practitioner.

'Something passed her . . .' See the comment above – an important stress in the structure of the novel.

Gulliver's Travels . . . **Lilliput** . . . **Brobdignag** The novel by Dean Swift (1667–1745) published in 1726, Lilliput being the land of the tiny people and Brobdignag (correctly Brobdingnag) the land of the giants.

lingerly i.e. lingeringly.

'My feet they are sore . . .' Note the comment above, since the poem is in effect a kind of theme song for the novel itself and the mental and physical journeys of the heroine.

enounced Said, spoke out.

backboards i.e. boards placed to keep the back straight.

Welsh rabbit i.e. rarebit, cheese mixed with egg, milk, etc. toasted on toast.

Chapter 4

Jane waits for news, the children largely ignoring her, though she hits John Reed and reminds Mrs Reed of her uncle Reed's wishes. She grows closer to Bessie and then, in mid-January, is sent for to see Mr Brocklehurst, who has come to arrange for her admission to Lowood School. His interrogation and Mrs Reed's comments punctuate the interview. Mrs Reed tells him that Jane is deceitful, but after he has gone Jane accuses her aunt of lying and certainly seems to frighten her in the process.

Commentary

Mrs Reed's tactics are calculated to produce a greater sense of isolation from her family in Jane, but with the recovery of her health Jane recovers her spirit too, and the ingrained sense of injustice gives her something of a triumph over Mrs Reed. She has the common childish idea that her mother and father can see what Mrs Reed is doing, and effectively uses it as spiritual and moral blackmail on that unscrupulous woman. There is pathos in Jane's account of how she is sustained by her love of her doll, and even in the occasional nocturnal visit of Bessie with food, and the rare kiss. Note the satirical account of the business acumen of Eliza Reed and the vanity of Georgiana, balanced by the hurrying of the apprehensive Jane to the breakfast-room. The child's-eye view of the 'black pillar' is convincing, the false Christianity of Brocklehurst contrasting with the factual common sense of Jane with her 'I must keep in good health, and not die'. Jane's independence is even shown by her unconventional preferences for certain Old Testament books in the Bible. Jane's suffering at Mrs Reed's public accusation is an anticipation of her suffering on a later occasion at Lowood. Note the emphasis on the mortification of the flesh, certainly not practised by either Brocklehurst (or his family) or by Mrs Reed and hers. There is something ludicrous in Brocklehurst referring to Lowood as 'that nursery of chosen plants'. The giving of the tract to Jane is also an un-Christian action. Jane's indictment of Mrs Reed is evidence of her courage and forthrightness and her poignant sense of the isolation and injustice with which she is treated. Jane's comment causes her to expand with triumph, but the aftermath again shows her sensitivity, 'its after-flavour, metallic and corroding'. Her seeking even the cold bleak air is natural after this, her frank avowal of affection for Bessie natural too. Jane has lost her shyness and even some of her sense of injustice, as we note from her 'Even for me life had its gleams of sunshine.'

supplied the hiatus by a homily i.e. filled the gap with a sermon.
a faded graven image An idol – see Exodus, xx,4.
traffic i.e. trade, bargaining.
poltroon Abject coward.
a black pillar . . . sable-clad . . . like a carved mask Note that the appearance and the images – black – are more devilish than Christian.
ruth Compassion.
port i.e. way of holding herself.
sotto voce Under the breath (Italian).
'onding on snaw' i.e. threatening a heavy fall of snow (dialect).

Chapter 5

Jane leaves Gateshead early in the morning and travels by stage coach the fifty miles to Lowood. Arriving there late at night, she is received by the superintendent, Miss Temple. Jane is too fatigued to eat, joins the other girls and teachers the next day, and endures a breakfast of burnt porridge. Miss Temple orders a lunch of bread and cheese to be served as recompense. Jane begins to look around her at Lowood, and makes the acquaintance of a girl who tells her about the nature of the institution. Later Jane observes the girl receiving a punishment.

Commentary

Fine creation of early-morning atmosphere opens this chapter, with Jane's excitement noted. At the beginning and the end of the journey this deprives her of an appetite. Note at once the kindness of Miss Temple, but also the realism in the description of Miss Miller and Jane's first reactions to the situation, particularly the ritual of communal discipline. The next day sees the beginning for Jane of the hard (but for her not harsh) rules of that discipline, the burnt porridge reflecting the abuse suffered by charity children in this particular establishment. Even in her appraisal thus early Jane shows her capacity for criticism, but she also shows her capacity for attachment (and of course her own need for love) in her feelings for Miss Temple and her talking to the girl whom we later come to know as Helen Burns. Note Miss Temple's practical Christianity in issuing the bread and cheese, and Helen Burns's influence on Jane, both with regard to the information she gives her but also because of the stoicism with which she accepts punishment.

dips Candles tapered in shape, made by repeatedly dipping the wicks into tallow or wax.

Babel clamour The Tower of Babel was built by the descendants of Noah, but their cunning design of uniting the world was destroyed by the confusion of languages therein (Genesis, xi, 9).

tucker Ornamental cloth to cover the chest.

the globes Spheres representing the earth, used in the teaching of geography.

organ of Veneration A reference to the science of phrenology, where the shape and formation of the head in each individual was related to their emotions and abilities.

irids Form of the plural of 'iris', the coloured part of the eye.

frieze Coarse woollen cloth.

prospect View.

Rasselas The novel written by Dr Johnson (1709–84) published in 1759, an essay on 'the choice of life'.

pelisses Long cloaks.

Revision questions on Chapters 1–5

1 Write an essay on the main characteristics of Jane's personality as they are revealed in these chapters.

2 Write brief character sketches of (a) John Reed (b) Mrs Reed and (c) Bessie.

3 How does Charlotte Brontë convey the fact that we are being shown events through a child's eyes? You may refer to any two or three incidents in your answer.

4 Compare and contrast Gateshead and Lowood from Jane's point of view.

5 Describe the part played by Miss Temple and Helen Burns in Jane's life so far.

Chapter 6

The next day is cold and the water is frozen. Jane is enrolled as a member of the fourth class, and she notices that 'Burns' is constantly being reprimanded by Miss Scatcherd. She is publicly caned, and on the evening of the same day Jane talks with her. Jane finds her clever and strange, as indeed she had done the previous day. Helen has learned to accept all her sufferings with endurance, though she feels certain things strongly, and she counsels Jane to 'do good to them that hate you and despitefully use you'. She tells Jane that life is too short for her to nurse wrongs against Mrs Reed.

Commentary

The atmosphere of cold signals the hardships ahead. Jane's natural curiosity draws her to Helen, and her sense of injustice on Helen's behalf is a tribute to the warmth of Jane's nature. The daily ritual of times and classes gives the first part of this chapter a documentary flavour, with its question and answer techniques and the system of rote-learning. The caning is an unpleasant reality, and Helen's failure to defend herself – she could not wash in view of the ice – smacks of masochism despite her explanation to Jane later. She is stoic though, and, as she says, she needs to secure her education. Her Christianity is certainly rooted in Biblical teaching, seen in her assertion that 'the Bible bids us return good for evil'. Helen is important in Jane's education, her doctrine of endurance and acceptance providing Jane with a new if at present unacceptable perspective. Ironically, Helen's public flogging is what Jane fears she could not endure – though she has to face public exposure when Brocklehurst visits the school. Helen believes in cleanliness and order and confesses her own faults, but she has a certain maturity which is revealed in her critical appraisal of Charles I. Helen moreover has a belief in the spirit, a faith in the after-life which is profoundly moving. Her faith and rationality combine to educate Jane, but Helen's lot is imbued with pathos, particularly when she observes that 'I live in calm, looking to the end'.

tonnage and poundage Taxes levied during Charles I's reign on goods entering the country: tonnage 7½p to 15p (worth much more then) on every tun of liquor, poundage from 2½p to 5p on every pound of dry goods.
ship-money A tax levied on seaport towns which Charles I reintroduced in 1634.
like Felix See Acts, xxiv, 25.
poor murdered king The execution of Charles I aroused popular feeling for the King and has continued to do so.

Chapter 7

Life at Lowood is described. It is particularly hard during the winter months when the girls suffer from chilblains, and when they long to get back to Lowood from church. When they do they are sometimes shut out from the fire by the bigger girls. One day Mr Brocklehurst, his wife and daughters pay a visit to the Institution. Mr Brocklehurst lectures Miss Temple on economy and vanity. Jane accidentally breaks her slate, thus drawing Mr Brocklehurst's attention to herself. He tells the whole school that Jane is a liar, tells the teachers to keep a special eye on her, and orders that she be punished by being placed on a stool for half an hour more. Jane is greatly comforted by the fact that Helen Burns smiles when she passes her and that another girl raises her eyes to her.

Commentary

The social documentary continues with the account of Sundays. There is some emphasis on degraded and run-down human nature – seen in the big girls commandeering food and warmth and the suffering of all in the cold, but also some compensatory faith in that human nature in the person and example of Miss Temple. Mr Brocklehurst's visit is a fine dramatic stroke: the language is still black, Brocklehurst is 'this piece of architecture', and Jane's imagination works overtime as she thinks that his conversation with Miss Temple is about her (Jane's) supposed infamy. Brocklehurst's idea of Christianity is the mortification of the flesh – except in his own family. His pronouncement on the bread and cheese meal is quite typical of his one-sided interpretation of Christianity. In short, he is a bigot, pompous, self-important, un-Christian, unfeeling, and on the question of curled hair, hypocritical and grotesque – 'we are not to conform to nature'. There is also something sadistic in his insistence on the cutting off of hair, and the entrance of his wife and daughters effectively confirms his hypocrisy. Note Miss Temple's kindness to Jane, Brocklehurst's severity and savage unfairness, and the magic moment when Jane realizes that she is not alone or despised.

the golden age i.e. when people were innocent of evil and therefore happy.

starved Perished with cold.

hebdomadal Weekly.

Eutychus See Acts xx, 9–12, where Paul restores to life Eutychus, who had fallen out of a window.

surtout Overcoat.

the 'Coming Man' See Matthew, xi, 3.

take up their cross . . . live by bread alone . . . if ye suffer hunger or thirst . . . Note that Brocklehurst refers constantly to the Bible for support – ironic in view of the un-Christian things he is advocating.

false front of French curls Artificial hair.

like a dagger Note the effective use of this image – almost a paradox in the circumstances.

like burning glasses Again the physical image to convey emotional suffering.

the Rubicon was passed The river between Gaul and Italy crossed by Julius Caesar with his army; thereafter he disregarded the laws of Rome and began his campaign against Pompey. General meaning is – there is no going back.

Brahma The Absolute and Supreme Being in the Hindu religion.

Juggernaut One name of the Hindu god Krishna, whose image was drawn in a chariot at Puri in Orissa, his worshippers throwing themselves under the wheels to be crushed and so reach Paradise.

Bethesda See John, v, 2. A pool in Jerusalem purported to have healing powers for the first person to enter it after its waters had been troubled.

Chapter 8

Jane is overwhelmed with grief but Helen reasons that if
Brocklehurst had treated her as a favourite she would certainly
have made enemies. Helen in fact continues to stress the after-
life rather than earthly reward. Miss Temple appears and takes
both Helen and Jane to her room. Jane tells her her story, and
Miss Temple decides to write to Mr Lloyd for confirmation. She
is obviously worried by Helen's cough and gives the girls a
'refreshing meal'. After a week has passed Miss Temple announ-
ces to the whole school that Jane is cleared of the imputation
against her.

Commentary

Jane's punishment is made the more ironic because she has been
making progress in the school. As always, she is extremely emotional (once again a stress on her need to be loved), and here
Helen shows her practical Christianity in trying to get her to eat
and her practical common sense in getting the Brocklehurst
punishment into perspective. Jane cries out her need for love,
and this moves Helen – certainly conscious of her own coming
death – to the utterance of her favourite theme: 'God waits only
the separation of spirit from flesh to crown us with a full
reward.' Jane's sensitivity moves her to sadness on Helen's
account. Miss Temple too exemplifies the true spirit of
Christianity and, in telling her story, Jane shows that she has
already profited from Helen's counsels of moderation. She also
shows that she has an enquiring mind and the need to acquire
learning when she listens to Miss Temple and Helen Burns. She
does not quite succeed in curbing her own indignation when
Helen wears the 'Slattern' badge round her neck.

gall and wormwood The bile produced from the liver and the plant
  are both bitter to the taste.
whalebone and iron i.e. a reference to her corsets and her character.
nectar and ambrosia The wine and food of the Gods in Greek
  mythology.
Virgil The great Latin poet (70–19 BC).
phylactery Passages of Jewish scripture written on parchment
  enclosed in skin and worn on the forehead. In Matthew xxiii, 5
  Pharisees are rebuked by God for wearing very broad phylacteries.
the Barmecide supper Barmecide, a prince, offered his guests supper

but in fact gave them nothing to eat. The story comes from *The Arabian Nights*.
Cuyp-like Albert Cuyp (1605–91), Dutch landscape painter.

Chapter 9

When spring comes the countryside around Lowood is very beautiful, but since the school lies in a hollow there is a general risk to health through the damp and fog. With the arrival of the warmer weather typhus breaks out, and many of the inhabitants are taken ill. Jane learns that Helen is seriously ill and not expected to live (she has consumption). One evening when she and a friend return Jane learns that Helen is much worse. That night Jane goes to find Helen and gets into bed with her. Helen tells Jane that she is going to God. The next morning the two children are discovered in each other's arms; Jane is asleep, but Helen is dead.

Commentary

Again we note the realism, with Jane's feet recovering in the spring and her expressing genuine delight in the countryside in its changed state. This is conveyed through the personification ('Lowood shook loose its tresses'), but this idyllic contemplation is changed by reality – the onset of typhus. Again Miss Temple displays her outstanding qualities of humanitarian dedication, but there is a considered stress on the incidence of death. Brocklehurst will not visit the school and, a terrible irony this, the healthy have more to eat because there are so many ill who cannot manage their food. Despite the fact that she learns much from the more experienced Mary Ann Wilson, Jane remains loyal to the memory of Helen. It says much for her courage and independence as well as her loyalty that she seeks Helen out. Their exchange is poignant with the certainty of approaching death for Helen; the pathos is such that we are moved by the contemplation of a brave death in which humility and the assurance of faith go hand in hand, as close in Helen's mind as she is close to Jane in her final hours.

auriculas Primroses.
beck Brook.
'ing' and holm Low-lying meadow and flat ground, respectively, by a river.

advert Refer to.
effluvia Decaying matter.
'Resurgam' I will arise (Latin).

Chapter 10

The typhus outbreak rouses public indignation about the conditions at Lowood, and the school is rebuilt and run on different and more enlightened lines. Jane stays there for another eight years, six as pupil and two as teacher. But after Miss Temple marries a clergyman and moves away Jane becomes unsettled; she contemplates the narrowness of her life at Lowood, and advertises for another post. She is now 'barely eighteen'. She receives a letter from a Mrs Fairfax of Thornfield Hall near Millcote, who wants her to undertake the tuition of one little girl. The committee of Lowood decides that Mrs Reed shall be consulted, but she washes her hands of Jane and the latter accordingly gets the testimonial she requires. On the night before she leaves Lowood Bessie comes from Gateshead to see her. She has married Robert, the coachman, and now has two children of her own. She brings Jane news of the Reed children, of Georgiana's failed elopement with a lord, which was frustrated by Eliza, and of John Reed's dissipation and his failing his examinations. Jane also learns that her uncle, a wine merchant from Madeira, had come to Gateshead nearly seven years before looking for his niece.

Commentary

This is a transition chapter, marking the passage of time, filling in the events prior to Jane's undertaking new employment. At the same time we note the directness of the narrative technique, the sense of social concern and a maturity of style consonant with the maturity of the narrator – particularly when she refers to 'those who knew how to combine reason with strictness, comfort with economy, compassion with uprightness'. Jane reveals her industry and ability, but she is still subject to extremes of emotion as, for example, when she spends the half-holiday granted on the occasion of Miss Temple's marriage in solitude. This solitude has immediate results, what Jane herself calls 'a transforming process' which makes her 'tired of the routine of eight years in one afternoon'. The wish for change – and the clear recognition that liberty will be new servitude – seems natural enough, but Jane is a creature of impulse and in this instance acts on it. There is a fine sense of tension in Jane's not being able to open the letter she receives immediately, a warm sense of loyalty and affection in Jane's welcoming Bessie. The latter's narrative serves to fill in necessary background, with the focus on the visit of Mr Eyre an important strand in the later unravelling of the plot.

brackish Salty.
post-chaise A closed four-wheeled horse-drawn mail coach.
sublunary i.e. worldly, earthly.
en règle Conventional (French).
mediatrix Mediator.
plucked Failed his examinations (slang).
Madeira One of a group of volcanic islands in the North Atlantic west of Morocco.

Revision questions on Chapters 6–10

1 Indicate the main differences in character between Jane and Helen Burns.

2 Write an account of life at Lowood both before and during the typhus epidemic.

3 Describe Mr Brocklehurst and his ideas of how Lowood Institution should be run.

4 Why did Jane decide to leave Lowood and how did she bring this into effect?

5 Write an essay on Jane's need to be loved as shown in these chapters.

Chapter 11

Jane arrives at the George Inn at Millcote where she is met by John, the coachman from Thornfield. He takes her to the Hall, where she meets Mrs Fairfax, whom she immediately likes. She learns that her pupil is called Adèle Varens. The next morning Mrs Fairfax explains that she is housekeeper to Mr Rochester, the owner of Thornfield, and that the child concerned is his ward. Jane meets Adèle, who talks mainly in French; later Jane is shown over the house by Mrs Fairfax. While they are in the attics they hear a strange laugh, which Mrs Fairfax says comes from one of the servants, Grace Poole. She calls out to Grace and scolds her for making too much noise.

Commentary

In this chapter we note a distinct assumption of the authorial tone – 'A new chapter in a novel ... Reader, though I look comfortably accommodated' – a reminder that we *are* reading a novel. As ever, Jane's imagination is very much alive as she is driven to Thornfield. Once there, she appreciates the atmosphere and responds to Mrs Fairfax warmly. The isolation and attendant loneliness of the house are stressed, and so relieved is Jane to find herself in a comfortable small bedroom that she offers up prayers of gratitude. Jane takes a pride in her appearance the next day, a pride that is free from vanity. She has an artist's pride, too, in visual description and perspective (this is part of Charlotte Brontë's style). Adèle proves to be spoiled and over-talkative, delighting in being the centre of attraction. Jane soon finds that she lacks application to her work. The account of the house is both visual and atmospheric, with great detail on furniture and decoration, while the laugh – and the supposed identification of Grace Poole – are important to the plot.

the death of Wolfe (1727–59) The General killed during his capture of Quebec in the war against the French (1756–63).
Happen Perhaps.
noan Not.
beau-ideal Perfect beauty (French), here 'perfection'.
negus Port and lemon juice, spiced and sweetened.
cuirass The breast-plate and back-plate of armour.
'C'est là ma gouvernante?' Is this my governess?
certainement Assuredly.
canzonette Little song (Italian).
'La Ligue des Rats, fable de La Fontaine' La Fontaine (1621–95). French poet and writer celebrated for his *Fables*. This one tells how the mouse, frightened of the cat, appeals to the rats for help. They come to attack, but run away when the cat looks at them.
Tyrian-dyed They were purple in colour, as if treated with the famous purple dye from Tyre in Palestine.
Parian Marble brought from the island of Paros in Greece.

Bohemian glass i.e. from Bohemia – now Czechoslovakia – famous through the centuries for its glass.

the Hebrew ark The small chest made by the Jews at God's command as the most sacred emblem of their religion. (See Exodus, xxv,10–22.)

'after life's fitful fever they sleep well' *Macbeth*, III, 2, 23: 'After life's fitful fever he sleeps well'.

Bluebeard's castle Bluebeard was the villain in a number of European folk tales who married several wives and murdered each of them.

cachinnation Loud and uncontrolled laughter.

'Mesdames, vous êtes servies . . .' 'Ladies, dinner is ready . . . I am very hungry.'

Chapter 12

Jane settles into the routine of life at Thornfield with Mrs Fairfax and Adèle, but at times she longs for a widening of her experience. There are occasions when she hears 'Grace Poole's laugh', but three uneventful months pass away until one day in January Jane sets out for the neighbouring village of Hay in order to post a letter. It is evening, Jane rests on a stile, and a man on horseback and a large dog pass her. The horse falls on the slippery road and Jane helps the man, who has sprained his ankle, to remount. She goes on to post her letter, returns to Thornfield and finds the large dog in Mrs Fairfax's room. One of the servants tells her that it is Mr Rochester's dog, and that Mr Rochester has arrived home after an accident.

Commentary

The chapter is virtually divided into two parts, the first being a focus on Jane's consciousness and the second the dramatic incident involving Rochester and its aftermath with Jane discovering who he is. Jane is restless at times, and we note an authorial assertion which shows how far in advance of her time Charlotte Brontë was. There is a strong feminist note in her 'but women feel just as men feel; they need exercise for their faculties, and a field for their efforts as much as their brothers do'. Dramatic tension is maintained by Jane hearing the laugh and the 'eccentric murmurs', and there is some fine, even poetic description, as when the birds 'looked like single russet leaves that had forgotten to drop'. The atmosphere generated by the 'Gytrash' moves from the supernatural to the realistic, witness the description of Rochester. His downright manner, a rough bluntness, is heightened by the fact that the reader, though not Jane, guesses who he is from his questioning of her. After the adventure Jane is excited enough to feel that her return to Thornfield is 'stagnation', but the narrative sweep of the chapter is such that Pilot's presence in the room and Leah's account of Rochester raise her tension and ours.

par parenthèse By way of an aside (French).

I am merely telling the truth Note the directness of this and how it contributes to the authenticity of Jane's experiences.

Revenez bientôt . . . Jeannette Come back soon, my dear friend, my dear Miss Jenny.

momently Momentarily.

as in a picture Note this, for Jane is an artist herself and this is an example of her thinking visually.

'Gytrash' North of England legend says that a spirit in the form of a horse, mule or dog haunts lonely paths and accosts belated travellers.

pretercanine More than dog-like, supernatural.

halted to Limped towards.

the mountain will never be brought to Mahomet . . . The prophet Mahomet asserted his claims to power and commanded Mount Safa to come to him. When it did not, Mahomet declared that God was merciful, since if the mountain had come it would have destroyed him. He said that he would go to the mountain and thank God for his mercy.

My help had been needed and claimed An important underlining of Jane's salient characteristic – the need to give and the need to be accepted and loved.

Chapter 13

On the day after Rochester's arrival Adèle proves troublesome. Her mind is running on presents, and later in the day she and Jane are invited to take tea with Rochester, who proves to be in a grumpy mood because of his riding accident. He questions Jane, is again abrupt, finds out all he can about her previous life, and then gets her to play the piano. He also looks over her portfolio of paintings and offers some criticism of them. Later Jane discusses Rochester with Mrs Fairfax, who tells her that Rochester inherited the property nine years before on the death of his elder brother Rowland, with whom he had quarrelled.

Commentary

Note the generation of excitement at Thornfield because of Rochester's presence and Adèle's essentially superficial character – understandable in a child – and expectation of a present. Jane now sees Rochester in his own small kingdom, and there is again a strong physical description of a powerful yet unidealized physical presence. He is both abrasive and formal though almost rude, his manner arresting to Jane and the reader alike. His eyes are 'dark, irate, and piercing', his bluntness and directness in questioning Jane shows his initial interest in her unusual qualities, though she outmanoeuvres him verbally by saying that she has received her 'cadeau' in the praise of Adèle's progress. There is something both light and passionate in the conversation, ranging from Rochester's association of Jane with the fairies and his rather jealous and impertinent suggestion that all the girls at Lowood must have worshipped Brocklehurst. Yet Rochester is aware of his authoritarian attitude. The account of the paintings reflects Jane's artistic and imaginative bent, the mixture of violent feeling and morbidity in her nature, with the cormorant a symbol of greed, the corpse perhaps her submerged self. The vision of the Evening Star anticipates Jane's later journey, while the third picture has a kind of surrealistic quality, the religious/spiritual expression being almost overlaid by the associations with death and cold. Rochester's criticism, though hard, reflects the calibre of his own mind and an acknowledgement, rather rudely expressed, of Jane's individuality. Mrs Fairfax's account of his past does much to integrate his character.

prenomens First names of Romans. Gaius is the prenomen of Gaius Julius Caesar.

'Et cela . . . mademoiselle?' 'That must mean that there is a present for me in it, and perhaps one for you also, Miss Eyre. [Mr Rochester] has spoken of you: he asked me the name of my governess, and if she was not short, rather thin, and a little pale. I said she was, for you are, aren't you, Miss Eyre?'

Heidelberg The famous German university town.

choler i.e. shortness of temper.

to accost her i.e. to demand her attention.

disembarrassed i.e. not embarrassed (as I should have been by over politeness).

'N'est-ce pas . . . coffre?' 'Isn't there a present for Miss Eyre in your little trunk, sir?'

consoles and chiffonnières Ornamental brackets and pieces of furniture with fitted drawers and shelves, sideboards.
the men in green Fairies.
eulogiums Praises, recommendations.
religieuses Nuns.
pass your word i.e. vouch for, swear by.
second i.e. support.
Latmos The mountain on which, in Greek mythology, Endymion was put to sleep by the goddess of the moon, who loved him.
brook Endure.

Chapter 14

Rochester seems much occupied with business, and Jane only sees him occasionally. He sends for her and Adèle one evening, and gives Adèle a box of presents, and while she is investigating these with Mrs Fairfax, Rochester talks further with Jane. The latter tries to remain in the shadow, but Rochester draws her forward. He surprises her into saying that he is not handsome, and continues to talk about his looks and his past in such an eccentric way that Jane feels he has been drinking. Jane, however, notices his pride in the way he carries himself. He insists that he wishes to know more of Jane, but she cannot advance topics; he claims his right to be masterful, Jane resists, and Rochester is moved to acknowledge that he has faults, talks of the temptations of his past life, and covertly watches the behaviour of Adèle.

Commentary

We note, as Jane does, Rochester's abrupt changes of mood, but we also note his very positive interest in Jane; he even shows his guests her portfolio. Rochester is sarcastic to Adèle, who is obviously intent on getting what she can out of him. Rochester is masterful towards Jane; yet she notices that in fact he is much more genial, and her own interest in him is evident from the warmth of her descriptions. He is sensitive about his appearance, yet there is a deliberate assertiveness in his display, almost as if he wants Jane to find him attractive. He is also sensitive about his past, but there is a kind of dramatic irony here, since the most important incident in that past (his marriage) is at this stage concealed from Jane and from us. It is clear that he is very taken with Jane's integrity, with her individuality; he is haughty and Jane is aware of his condescension, though he stresses his age difference, and is moved to confess – here vaguely – his past. He is certain that Jane is a good listener, even asserting that this may be her future role in life, to listen to the confidences of others. Rochester gets good advice from Jane, who doesn't quite follow his vagaries of mood and address, but Rochester has the last word in his half-revelation about Adèle's mother and his determination to follow the 'principle of expiating numerous sins, great or small, by one good work'.

rencontre Meeting.

petit coffre Little trunk.

Ma boîte My box.

tiens-toi tranquille . . . Keep quiet, child, do you understand?

Oh, ciel! . . . Oh, how lovely it is!

auditress and interlocutrice i.e. listen to her and talk to her.

nonnette Young nun *or* a small bird. In view of Rochester's later image of Jane in this chapter, he obviously means both.

intellectual organs . . . sign of benevolence See note on phrenology earlier, p.28.

port i.e. way of carrying himself.

intrinsic or adventitious Qualities which are natural and those which are acquired.

et j'y tiens My mind will not be changed.

hector Bully, from Hector, the Trojan hero.

forte Strong point.

neophyte Novice.

I am paving hell with energy . . . good intentions An adaptation of the proverbial 'The road to hell is paved with good intentions.'

law . . . of the Medes and Persians Unalterable laws – Daniel vi,12.

Sphynx The stone monster at Thebes was supposed to put riddles to travellers and destroy those who could not answer them.

a curious sort of bird through the close-set bars of a cage . . . The image is directed at the real Jane, but the terrible irony is that Rochester's mad wife is imprisoned in the attic-cage above unknown to Jane.

'Il faut que . . . même' 'I must try it on at once.'

on the boards i.e. on stage.

'Est-ce que ma robe va bien . . .' 'Does my dress look nice? And my shoes and stockings? I believe that I am going to dance.'

chasséed i.e. in a kind of gliding dance-step.

'Monsieur, je vous remercie . . .' 'Mr Rochester, I thank you a thousand times for your kindness. That's what mamma would do, isn't it?'

grass green i.e. ignorant, innocent.

Chapter 15

Mr Rochester talks a great deal to Jane, and one day he tells her Adèle's story. The latter is the daughter of Céline Varens, an opera-dancer who had been Rochester's mistress. Rochester discovered that she had another lover, and he fought a duel with him. Rochester is not certain that Adèle is his daughter, but when her mother later abandoned her he decided to bring her up. Later that night as Jane thinks about what she has learned, she knows that Rochester still appeals to her, that she values him more than anything else despite his faults. She ponders on whether he will leave Thornfield. She hears movements and the 'demoniac laugh' as well as gurgles and moans, gets up to investigate and finds that Rochester's room is on fire. She drenches him and the hangings round the bed, and thus saves his life. He asks her to say nothing about the incident to Mrs Fairfax, leaves her for a while, and then returns, seizing on Jane's belief that the laugh she heard came from Grace Poole. He seems on the point of saying more – perhaps even confessing his love to Jane, who has saved his life – but does not commit himself.

Commentary

It is a measure of Rochester's feelings for Jane that he confides his past to her, perhaps seeking security in her reactions to it. Rochester's own narrative is exciting and direct, with the description of the rocks and the stream conveying the varying experiences of life. His praise of Thornfield and 'I like the sternness and stillness of the world under this frost' show his strength and his uncertainty, the tough, brave quality of his mind and physique. But there are also a number of clues to his fear, and concealment costs him much tortured emotion, his glance at Thornfield showing the variety of suffering. There is a refreshing frankness about his narration and, afterwards, Jane even pets Adèle, almost out of sympathy for her situation. As she considers Rochester she notes the consistency of his present behaviour towards her, and she notes also the improvement in her own health and spirits, signs, we suspect, of her falling in love. It is touching to note Jane's faith in Rochester's inherent goodness. The whole of the fire incident is graphic narrative, immediate, exciting, tense with danger and mystery. Jane's susceptibility continues through the night, and indeed she may sense that Rochester is not merely grateful but perhaps on the way to being in love with her.

'grande passion' Great love, infatuation.
'taille d'athlète' physique of an athlete.
Apollo Belvidere Famous statue of the god of music and the arts in the court of Belvedere in the Vatican.
Gallic sylph . . . British gnome This derives from the Rosicrucian theory put forward in an eighteenth-century book that the four elements of earth, air, fire and water are inhabited by gnomes, sylphs, salamanders, and nymphs.
hotel Mansion.
dentelles Lace.
spoony Romantic fool.
bonbons Gifts (sweets).
croquant Crunching.
'voiture' Carriage.
opera inamorata Opera-girl mistress.
Mon ange My angel.
porte cochère Courtyard gate.
a hag like one of those . . . See *Macbeth* Act I, Scene 1.
Job's Leviathan See Job xli for the description of an animal not known to modern naturalists, but almost certainly of immense size.
roué . . . vicomte A debauched viscount.
beauté mâle Manly attraction.
meeting i.e. the duel.
fillette Daughter, girl.
crescent-destiny i.e. the moon (seen as controlling fate).
fulminating strange anathemas i.e. cursing loudly about things.
sweet as the hills of Beulah See Isaiah, lxii. The name given to Israel in allegory, meaning 'spouse' and implying that Israel is united with God. It is the land of great happiness in John Bunyan's *Pilgrim's Progress* (1678).

Revision questions on Chapters 11–15

1 Write an account of Jane's first impressions of Thornfield and of her early days there.

2 Indicate clearly how Charlotte Brontë maintains narrative tension throughout these chapters.

3 In what ways is Rochester an unusual character? You should refer closely to the text in your answer.

4 In what ways does Charlotte Brontë make use of the past in these chapters?

5 Write an essay on *either* (a) the fire *or* (b) Jane's paintings *or* (c) Adèle.

Chapter 16

The next morning Jane is apprehensive, but she hears a conversation indicating that Rochester has accounted for the fire by saying that he was reading in bed. She sees Grace Poole, puts her to the test, but obtains no information and feels that the woman is behaving brazenly. At tea Jane is disappointed to learn that Rochester has gone on a visit to Mr Eshton who lives on the other side of Millcote. Mrs Fairfax describes the ladies whom he will meet there, mentioning especially the beautiful Blanche Ingram. After the account Jane takes herself severely to task for even daring to imagine that she could ever have been a favourite with Rochester.

Commentary

The chapter is concerned with two main elements – the aftermath of the fire and Jane's interrogation of Grace Poole, followed by her learning of Blanche Ingram. The first part reflects Jane's determination to find out what she can and to incriminate the woman 'who had attempted murder' in her own mind. At this point there is strong dramatic reaction, largely because of the coolness of Grace Poole and her phlegmatic repeating of the story that Rochester has obviously put about. She also manages to make Jane feel apprehensive by cross-questioning her in turn so that Jane suspects Grace of planning something against her. The narrative power concentrates on the sense of mystery in Jane's reactions to Grace Poole's 'miraculous self-possession and most inscrutable hypocrisy'. She even suspects that Grace may be blackmailing Rochester. The second part of the chapter finds Jane seized by a fit of inferiority. She learns of Rochester's social talents, has from Mrs Fairfax a description of Blanche Ingram which contrasts sharply to her own appearance, and uses her own inward monologue to establish a perspective of her feelings and her chances. It is summed up in the proposed self-portrait 'of a Governess, disconnected, poor, and plain'. It is perhaps typical of Jane's resilience, character, imagination *and* determination that she paints the two portraits she said she would – the one of herself and of the imagined and envied Blanche Ingram.

plate-closet i.e. where the valuable plates would be kept.
'Qu'avez-vous, mademoiselle . . .' 'What's the matter, Miss Eyre? Your fingers are trembling like a leaf and your cheeks are as red as cherries!'
entailed i.e. an estate which must pass to a certain heir and this cannot be altered by a will.
Arraigned at my own bar . . . Note the image. Jane is a great one for justice and injustice, and often thinks in these terms.
ignis-fatuus-**like** i.e. like a will o' the wisp.

Chapter 17

While Mr Rochester is away Jane continues to think about him, but sternly represses her feelings on the grounds that she can be nothing to him. After a fortnight Mrs Fairfax receives a letter announcing his return with a house-party. The preparations for this get under way, and Jane overhears the servants talking about the fact that Grace Poole gets more money than any of them. The guests arrive, and Jane now has the opportunity to observe Blanche Ingram. She also has to cope with Adèle for most of the evening while the guests dine. On the next day the company visits a site in the neighbourhood, and in the evening Jane is told to bring Adèle to the drawing-room after dinner. Jane sits in a corner, and describes the company, foremost among these being Lady Ingram and her daughters Blanche and Mary. Lady Ingram and Blanche converse very rudely on the faults, stupidities and inferiority of governesses. Jane watches the company and compares Rochester, much to his advantage, with each of them. After much badinage between Rochester and Blanche Ingram, she consents to play and he sings for her. Jane leaves after this, but meets Rochester outside the dining-room door. He tells her that she is depressed and is about to say more, but breaks off.

Commentary

There is a sense of expectation caused by Rochester's absence and then the news of the arrival of the house-party. Note the secret-cum-mystery of Grace Poole's wages and the effect of the preparations on Adèle who is, naturally, over-excited. The sense of social importance and ceremony is graphically observed when the party arrives. The effect of this is to increase Adèle's excitement and Jane's difficulties in managing her. Jane feels apprehensive about appearing in such elegant society, but gives an effective, direct, sometimes lightly satirical account of each member of the company. The Dowager Lady Ingram perhaps comes in for oblique condemnation because of her haughtiness and her 'fierce' and 'hard eye'. Blanche naturally draws Jane's longest critical look, and is herself satirical as well as haughty, self-conscious, accomplished but certainly not good-natured. The style switches to the graphic present in order to convey the immediacy of the scene. Jane's notice of Rochester, her dwelling on the detail of himself and his actions, all reflect 'an influence that quite mastered me – that took my feelings from my own power and fettered them in his'. Despite the social situation, Jane feels at one with him in essence, in spirit, in sympathy, and acknowledges her love for him to herself. Lady Ingram's and Blanche's comments on governesses – and well they know that Jane is within earshot – are vulgar, ill-bred, condescending, insensitive – and doubtless Rochester is intent on having them condemn themselves out of their own mouths. Miss Ingram certainly also reveals a sadistic quality. Both are uncomplicated snobs. Blanche is intent on creating the greatest possible impression, though her remarks about what her future husband will be like are ill-judged in Rochester's presence. Rochester's concern for Jane is apparent, as is the fact that he is measuring her integrity against the 'social graces' of Blanche and her mother.

'passées' Jaded.
chimeras i.e. grotesque products of the imagination.
list Made from the selvage of cloth.
laying by Saving.
Some natural tears she shed An echo of *Paradise Lost* Book XII, line 645 (Some natural tears they dropped, but wiped them soon) as Adam and Eve leave Eden.
'Elles changent . . .' 'They are changing their dresses.'
'Chez maman . . . apprend' 'When I was with my mother and people came to visit her, I used to follow them everywhere; to the drawing-room and to their bedrooms; I would often watch the ladies' maids do the hair of their mistresses and dress them, and it was so amusing. One learns from these things.'
'Mais oui . . . mangé' 'Oh yes, Miss Eyre. It is five or six hours since we had anything to eat.'
Abigails See note p.24.
victualage Food, provisions.
'et alors quel dommage!' 'And then what a pity!'
member i.e. of Parliament.

'Est-ce que . . . toilette' May I take just one of those wonderful flowers, Miss Eyre? Only to complete my outfit.

'minois chiffonné' With charmingly irregular features.

like a Dian i.e. after Diana, the Roman goddess of hunting.

coffee is brought in Note the historic present tense, which makes the descriptions real and immediate.

sparks i.e. young men about town.

père noble de théâtre Dressed according to the actors' idea of how a distinguished man should look.

incubi i.e. terribly burdensome.

'Tant pis!' So much the worse.

charivari Discordant noise, usually a mock serenade.

stick . . . blades Society slang for 'man' and 'dashing young men'.

la belle passion Love.

quiz Tease.

an abstract of the memoirs . . . Charlotte Brontë's own irony – Jane Eyre's 'Autobiography' constitutes just such a set of memoirs.

Signior Eduardo . . . Donna Bianca i.e. their names in Italian.

Rizzio . . . Mary . . . Bothwell David Rizzio, secretary to Mary, Queen of Scots, was murdered by the Earl of Darnley, her husband. Later, after Darnley had also been murdered, Mary was kidnapped by James Hepburn, Earl of Bothwell, whom she afterwards married.

Corsair-song i.e. a song about pirates, 'The Corsair' being the title of a poem by Lord Byron.

'con spirito' i.e. with animation.

'Gardez-vous en bien' 'Take care.'

Chapter 18

The house-party continues, and when a period of wet weather occurs the guests soon find indoor amusements. One evening they play charades. Jane, who has admitted to herself her love for Rochester, watches the various tableaux and particularly notes the behaviour of Rochester in relation to Blanche Ingram. She feels sure that Rochester will marry Blanche for family reasons. At the same time Jane notes that Blanche is failing to captivate Rochester. One day Rochester goes away on business, and a Mr Mason arrives from the West Indies. He claims to be an old friend of Rochester's. Just after this a gipsy arrives and insists on telling the ladies their fortunes. Blanche is obviously put out by what he tells her, and the chapter ends with Jane going to the library to have her fortune told.

Commentary

The charades are used to display Rochester's talents (and the imposing nature of Miss Ingram), but there is also an ironic forecasting of what is to happen in life in such a phrase as 'the pantomime of a marriage'. It is also ironic that Blanche, who at this stage wishes to be Rochester's bride, could not, of course, marry him. Rochester's acting here looks forward immediately to his convincing acting as the gipsy, while his prisoner role perhaps unconsciously reflects the prisoner in the attic – his own wife. Rochester in effect teases Blanche although she does not know it – 'we were married an hour since, in the presence of all these witnesses'. We note Jane's clear-sightedness with regard to the relationship between Blanche and Rochester, and her unswerving if partisan analysis of Blanche's character and her perform-ance (I choose the word deliberately) in setting out to captivate Rochester. Blanche is arrogant and certainly lacking in common humanity, qualities which Rochester appreciates so much in Jane. Not only is Jane clear-sighted here, she is also down-to-earth in her appraisal of upper-class motivation towards the *right* kind of marriage, that is, one which is commercially desirable or suitable because of birth. She also, however, observes Rochester closely, and sees that he is disturbed, something which in fact accounts for his departure and his coming disguise. Jane registers intuitively her suspicions of Mason, and notes the company's response to the gipsy – either that she is a source of fun or that she should be expelled immediately. Blanche rules autocratically but lives to regret it after her meeting with the gipsy; the other girls giggle at what she knows of them (a sure sign that she is an impostor) and Jane, unabashed, goes in, thus concluding the chapter on a note of tension.

halcyon sunshine 'Halcyon' is Greek for kingfisher, and symbolizes days of happiness.

charades Charades were popular among the middle and upper classes in the eighteenth and nineteenth centuries. A word was chosen, a group went outside and after brief rehearsal returned to act it, the rest of the company having to guess it.

Paynim Pagan.

'She hasted, let down her pitcher . . .' See Genesis xxiv, 20.

Eliezer and Rebecca See Genesis xv and xxiv.

Bridewell The house of correction, a prison, which existed in London near Blackfriars Bridge until 1864.

Levantine From the Levant, Eastern Mediterranean.
'Voilà Monsieur Rochester . . .' 'Here is Mr Rochester coming back . . .'
intelligence News.
girandoles Chandeliers with branches.
Mother Bunches Witches or old women.
crock Earthen pot.
beldame Old woman or hag.
tinkler Gipsy.
'le cas' i.e. a suitable occasion.
the old gentleman Satan or the devil.
Sybil An old woman with the gift of prophecy.
vinaigrettes Small perforated boxes of gold or silver used in the
  eighteenth century to hold smelling salts.

Chapter 19

Jane is down-to-earth and lacking in nervous excitement in her confrontation with the gipsy, though she starts when Grace Poole's name is mentioned. The gipsy further pursues the theme of marriage in relation to Rochester's guests and in particular his marriage to Blanche Ingram. The gipsy reveals that she has told Blanche Ingram something about Rochester's estate which should give her cause for concern. Further analysis of Jane's character follows, and then the gipsy reveals 'herself' as Rochester. He questions her about the company, and she tells him of Mason's arrival. This shocks him, and she gives him her support; later she gets him some wine and sends Mason to him. She hears him when they go to bed, and he sounds more cheerful.

Commentary

Rochester's thin disguise is only acceptable because of his brilliant performance in the charades. The dialogue with Jane even before his revelation of identity is spiced with his probing and contradictory tone and with her rational replies. Yet there is also something a little sadistic in this questioning of Rochester's, which seems to be testing Jane and her responses to his current situation. The revelation of what 'she' has said to Blanche almost gives the game away, and the mannered examination of Jane's features is as detailed as Jane's has been of his. Once the revelation has been made, Rochester's dependence on Jane is evident, particularly after her revelation in turn, when he says 'Jane, I've got a blow; I've got a blow, Jane!'

Sybil See note p.49.
nichered Neighed, laughed shrilly.
diablerie Devilry.
black-aviced Dark-complexioned.
rent-roll Rents from his properties.
dished Superseded.
still small voice See 1 Kings, xix, 12.
ad infinitum Without end (Latin).
Did I wake or sleep? An echo of the final line of Keats' 'Ode to a
  Nightingale'.
old Old age.
Off, ye lendings! Quoted from Shakespeare's *King Lear*, Act III,
  Scene 4.
ministrant i.e. ministering.

Chapter 20

Jane awakes in the night and hears a terrible cry. Soon there are
shouts for help and for Rochester, and Jane quickly goes to
investigate, finding the guests gathering together in great agi-
tation. Miss Ingram goes to Rochester, but he tells them that the
cause of all the noise is that a servant has had a nightmare. When
they have returned to their rooms he tells Jane to accompany
him to the upper floor. There she finds Mason collapsed, his
arm soaked in blood. Jane stays with him while Rochester goes to
fetch the surgeon. Nearby she hears an animal-like snarling and
the laugh she associated with Grace Poole. When Rochester
returns the surgeon dresses the wound and then departs with
the patient, though not before Mason has made some enigmatic
remarks. Rochester takes Jane into the garden and asks her
whether a man who has made a dreadful error and been sinful
has any right to defy the opinion of society and have a relationship with someone who can give him peace of mind. When he
speaks of Blanche Ingram he says that she might regenerate him
with a vengeance. He asks Jane if she will talk with him on the
night before he is married.

Commentary

The chapter opens with a dramatic and again violent and mysterious incident. Note the narrative directness, the graphic words
which Jane hears, the speed with which Rochester acts, the force
and authoritative directness of his presence. Such is Jane's sym-

pathetic affinity for Rochester that she expects him to call upon her; she shows firmness and courage in dealing with the situation (notice how dependent Rochester has become upon her) and there is increasing tension as Jane is left with the wounded man. A repeated series of 'I must' shows how Jane nerves herself for the ordeal, and another series of questions shows how Jane is completely absorbed in the mystery and the horror of what she has heard and, barely, seen. Mason's account of what happened when the surgeon is dressing his wound tells just enough to keep us, the readers, on the edge of the mystery too – can he really have been savaged by Grace Poole? Rochester continues to assert his authority, virtually forcing Mason to drink his concoction. There is a superb sense of contrast when Rochester and Jane go into the garden – the claustrophobic interior replaced by the freshness and air, intrigue replaced by freedom and a kind of innocence – though Rochester gives hints of his own uncertain state and fear of discovery. He appears to be undertaking an oblique confession of his own past to Jane. He is also making an oblique declaration of love and, in a way, asking for her consent in indulging it. There is, it must be admitted, something cloying in Jane's subservience, something teasing in Rochester's praise of Blanche Ingram – 'A strapper – a real strapper, Jane: big, brown and buxom' – and something a little sadistic too.

condor A large South American vulture.
Much Ado About Nothing The comedy by Shakespeare which is notable for the wit of Beatrice and Benedick (1599).
volatile salts Usually known as sal volatile.
Luke . . . St John's . . . Judas . . . Satan Note the range – typical of Jane's imagination – for she fears the evil present in the house and is summoning her Christian fortitude to combat it.
as a thunderbolt might fall on an oak A brilliantly unobtrusive image which (a) anticipates what does happen and (b) prefigures the physical shattering of Rochester much later.
cannily Cleverly.
charlatan Quack, fake.
hem Cough.
to stand on a crater-crust . . . It is an apt choice of image, since the volcano of concealment does erupt when he is about to marry Jane – and there is the later eruption of the fire which disfigures Rochester.
Ariel The spirit who serves Prospero and ultimately gains his freedom in Shakespeare's *Tempest*.

Revision questions on Chapters 16–20

1 Write an account of the charades and the entertainment at Thornfield Hall after the arrival of the guests.

2 Write a character-sketch of Blanche Ingram as she appears in these chapters.

3 In what ways do you find the gipsy scene (a) convincing and (b) unconvincing? You should refer closely to the text in your answer.

4 Show how Charlotte Brontë deepens the mystery of Thornfield. You should refer closely to the text.

5 How far do you feel sympathetic to or impatient with Jane?

6 What are the chief ingredients of Charlotte Brontë's narrative art in these chapters? Give examples in quotation to support your statements.

Chapter 21

Jane has a number of dreams about a little child. One afternoon she receives a visit from John, the coachman at Gateshead, who has been sent by Bessie to bring Jane to see Mrs Reed. The latter is seriously ill, and keeps asking for Jane. Jane learns that John Reed has committed suicide. Before she leaves Thornfield, Jane suggests to Rochester that when he marries Miss Ingram, Adèle should be sent to school as she will be seeking a new position. Jane returns to her aunt's house, talks to Bessie, and meets the now plump and pleasure-loving Georgiana, and Eliza, who is devoted to church works. Jane goes to see Mrs Reed and, just before she dies, the latter gives her a letter that had come three years before from her uncle, John Eyre, of Madeira, who expressed the wish to adopt his niece and to leave her his fortune. Mrs Reed confesses she so disliked Jane that she wrote to Mr Eyre saying that she (Jane) had died in the typhus epidemic at Lowood. Jane forgives her, Mrs Reed will not respond to her, and Eliza utters a glib comment but is moved at the end.

Commentary

Another transitional chapter, as the reader is taken from the tension and temperature of Thornfield to the changed circumstances of

Mrs Reed. We note Jane's superstitious nature, in that dreaming of a child is held to be a sign of trouble, and Jane has to leave Thornfield – trouble and yet, curiously, a fortuitous escape at this moment. Brilliantly the child is also associated – and this is part of the sub-text of the novel – with (a) the loss of Adèle and (b) Jane's wish-fulfilment of having a child (and hence, subconsciously, marriage to Rochester). The story is dramatic and moral, the death of John Reed underlining the fact that we get what we deserve. Mrs Reed's stroke reinforces this. Her guilt is understandable and reflects her shaken nature. Jane has to have the courage to disturb Rochester's guests in order to get permission to go, and Miss Ingram further endears herself to us by her eyes' comment on Jane ('What can the creeping creature want now?'). We note Rochester's possessiveness over Jane, his attempts to take a more affectionate farewell (despite his gruff, even abrasive, manner); we note Jane's reactions to the changed circumstances, and the changes in the sisters, each as bad as the other because of their self-indulgence, the one of society ambition, the other of religiosity. Mrs Reed gives much detail on her reason for rejecting Jane earlier, and it is also apparent that her mind is unhinged, since she thinks that John is still alive. Jane reveals her love for Rochester in the sketch she makes of him, while the sisters reveal their respective pettiness in condemnation of each other. The letter from John Eyre, and of course its concealment, is important to the plot. Jane reveals her true Christianity (compare this with Eliza's) in her forgiveness, but we are aware of the terrible pathos of Mrs Reed's lonely and unloved death – perhaps Jane has more feeling for her at the end than her daughters.

hearty Healthy.
pass Give.
purloined Stolen.
Cairngorm Rock crystal of a brownish-yellow colour found in the Cairngorms, a mountain group in Scotland.
pelisse See note p.28.
'quiz' i.e. a puzzling or eccentric individual.
switch Of wood, used as a cane.
sharpers Swindlers, cheating gamblers.
vignettes Small illustrations.
a naiad's head The head of a water-nymph of classical times.
a volume of ... fashionable life Note the ironic tone – obviously Charlotte despised the superficial, 'silver-fork' (society) novels of the period.

'the Rubric' Directions for the church service given in the Book of Common Prayer (Church of England) and formerly printed in red (hence the name).

remittent Casual.

competency i.e. sufficient to live on.

Chapter 22

Jane has been away from Thornfield for a month. Eliza and Georgiana in their separate ways wish her to stay longer. Soon Georgiana leaves (she later marries a man of fashion) and so Eliza too does, deciding to become a novice in a French convent. Jane returns to Thornfield, but does not know what will happen to her after that. When she arrives she is greeted by Rochester, who reprimands her for coming on foot; he also teases her about 'Mrs Rochester', though in fact there is no news about his coming marriage. He does not go to Ingram Park.

Commentary

Eliza and Georgiana fulfil what each considers her destiny, each an extreme, the one of hedonistic conduct, the other of ostentatious self-denial. One gets the impression that each is lonely in her own way. Jane's uncertainty is stressed throughout her journey to Thornfield and her arrival there, and note how her dream of Blanche Ingram shutting the gates of Thornfield against her is a revelation of her deepest fears. Though the haymaking symbolizes harvest and a happier future, an ugly image of parting which Jane calls 'a new-born agony – a deformed thing which I could not persuade myself to own and rear' blights her return. Nevertheless Rochester has obviously missed her, and there are times when we feel some impatience with Jane as she fails to spot the signs of his genuine interest in her. Jane, Adèle, Mrs Fairfax form what is really a family group, but still we – and Jane – are on the edge of uncertainty. She becomes depressed, but Rochester seems to be happy, and is certainly kind to Jane – 'never had I loved him so well'.

unknown bourne Another echo of *Hamlet* – see note p.24.

the tenets of Rome i.e. Catholicism.

cynosure i.e. focus of all eyes (in a ballroom).

vicinage Neighbourhood.

ignis fatuus See note p.45.
Queen Boadicea She ruled the British tribe the Iceni, who defied the
  Romans when they invaded her land (now Norfolk) and took poison to
  avoid torture by them (62 AD).
'prête à croquer . . .' Ready to eat her little English mother.

Chapter 23

As Jane walks in the orchard on Midsummer Eve she is discovered by Mr Rochester who, after some conversation, tells her
that he intends to take her up on her suggestion that Adèle
should go to school. He tells her that she must leave Thornfield,
and says that he has found a suitable post for her in Ireland.
There follows a long and teasing conversation in which Jane is
greatly moved and shows it; Rochester wrestles with himself, but
the result is that he asks Jane to marry him. At first incredulous,
she comes to accept that he means what he says. She consents,
but later in the night the horse-chestnut under which they had
been sitting is struck by lightning.

Commentary

There is considerable tension in Jane's garden-walk, since she is
intent on avoiding Rochester but cannot do so. When Rochester
reveals that he has eyes in the back of his head Jane, seeking an
excuse to leave him (she is somewhat puritanical), finds that she
cannot control her voice when he says that he is to marry
Blanche and that she must leave. The reader suspects dif-
ferently, but Jane apparently does not. Once more Rochester
appears to take some pleasure in teasing her, and once again
Jane is not acute enough to see what he is doing. All this makes
for narrative tension. Jane does give away her own feelings for
Thornfield and, of course, for her master (I use the term
deliberately in view of his command of the situation), and
becomes sobbingly impassioned, an unusual release for her. It
precipitates Rochester's confession of love (concealment of the
reality causes him to 'set his teeth'), and it is surprising that Jane
lets him kiss her though, typically, she tries to free herself.
There is a terrible irony when Rochester proposes and Jane says
'you have already made your choice' – little knowing that this is
true though not as she means it. When she adds 'Your bride
stands between us' we understand Rochester's assertive claiming

of this bride whose sanity is in no way in doubt and whose emotions are subjective to his every wish. At this stage, of course, neither we nor Jane know this. The ensuing scene is fraught with both their feelings – Jane is weaned from 'Sir' to 'Edward' – but the ominous incident of the chestnut tree is symbolic of what is to befall Rochester *and* (temporarily) the love of Jane and Rochester, so shortly to be struck by the lightning of disclosure. There is a neat, almost comic, touch in Mrs Fairfax's witnessing Rochester's passionate kissing of Jane.

Albion This is the old name for England.
'Day its fervid fires had wasted' The fifth line of Thomas Campbell's poem 'The Turkish Lady'.
the organ of Adhesiveness Another reference to the science of phrenology.
"flying away home" 'Ladyclock' is the Northern name for Ladybird, and this is part of the first line of the proverbial rhyme.

Chapter 24

The next morning Jane is warmly greeted by Rochester. He calls her 'Jane Rochester' and dwells on her beauty, much to Jane's embarrassment, telling her that they are going to travel. Their talk is light and happy, and Jane persuades Rochester to tell the truth about Blanche Ingram. He says that 'I feigned courtship of Miss Ingram because I wished to render you as madly in love with me as I was with you'. Jane is certainly madly in love with him now. She tells Mrs Fairfax of their forthcoming marriage, and that good woman is concerned in case the whole affair is merely a passing whim on Rochester's part. She urges Jane to keep Rochester at a distance, but Jane is irritated by this. She is somewhat worried by Rochester's desire to buy her jewels and fine clothes when he takes her and Adèle to Millcote. She spends an evening with him and he sings her a moving song, but she realizes that Mrs Fairfax is right and that she must keep control of Rochester. She wants to be a companion to her future husband, not a slave.

Commentary

Note that Jane's initial happiness is complemented by the beautiful June day, and even Mrs Fairfax's reserve – brought about by what she had seen the previous evening – cannot put her down. She is even quietly humorous in response to Rochester's compliments to her eyes. Yet Jane feels some fear of the future, almost as if her intuition is stronger than present happiness. Rochester's praise of her as a beauty (which she is not) shows how much in love with her he is, but Jane is sensitive to the truth, and realizes that such love must be based on reality and not infatuation. She is eminently reasonable about the nature of man's love. The feigned courtship of Blanche Ingram by Rochester reflects the man – passionate, jealous, what Jane calls eccentric, but it is more than these. There is a certain lack of principle here, consistent with his later behaviour of trying to ensure his marriage to Jane despite the fact that his wife is living. Note the effective contrast – and good influence – of Mrs Fairfax, her sense of status, of like responding to like, casting some doubts on the coming marriage. She also has a prophetic insight into what may happen to spoil things. Adèle's being allowed to go with Rochester and Jane on the expedition shows what power she does have over him, and this is reinforced by the story of the fairy. Jane has no false vanity, and dislikes the idea of clothes and jewellery; she also has independence, wishing that she had some fortune (from her uncle) so that she could repay Rochester. The eastern terminology of Rochester makes Jane aware of the need to assert her qualities of real companionship and love as distinct from being a kept woman – all this is ironic – or, in her own words, 'I will not be your English Céline Varens.' Jane is careful and plans how to behave, replacing the intimacy of the tête-à-tête by requesting a song. Rochester obliges, and the song is resonant with plot and situation echoes. It is expressive of Rochester's love and of Jane's consent to marry him, but it also has a teasing ambiguity, for 'My love was sworn, with sealing kiss,/With me to live – to die' goes beyond marriage – and Jane, as we shall see, is only prepared to go as far as marriage. When she later leaves Thornfield, though, she is in a sense dead to Rochester. Jane fights her feelings, as she has done so often in the past and will do in the future – and her keeping Rochester at bay here is prophetic of her dealing just as firmly with him in the future.

mustard-seed One of the fairies in *A Midsummer Night's Dream* – Rochester often refers to Jane as a fairy.

Hercules and Samson The first a son of Zeus, one of the chief heroes of Greek legend, who had to perform the twelve labours. His wife gave him the shirt of Nessus which, she believed, would make him love her again. It poisoned him. Samson was of great strength. He was betrayed by Delilah, who told the Philistines that his strength lay in his hair. (See Judges xvi–xvii.)

gild refined gold A quotation from Shakespeare's *King John*, Act IV, Scene 2.

king Ahasuerus The king of Persia, of great wealth, in the sixth century BC.

you had given the world for love, and considered it well lost The sentence is an echo of the title of Dryden's play (about Antony and Cleopatra) called *All for Love, or The World Well Lost* (1678).

'all is not gold that glitters' Proverbial phrase, used by Shakespeare in *The Merchant of Venice* and by Thomas Gray in 'Ode on the Death of a Favourite Cat, Drowned in a Tub of Gold Fishes'.

'sans mademoiselle' i.e. without Miss Eyre.

manna Food sent from Heaven to the Jews during their wanderings in the wilderness (Exodus xvi).

'Oh, qu'elle . . . confortable' Oh, how uncomfortable she will be!

'un vrai menteur' A real fibber.

'Contes de fée' Fairy-tales.

Danae She was the Princess of Argos in Greek mythology, wooed by Zeus in a golden shower after she had been imprisoned in a brazen tower by her father.

seraglio The wives and concubines of the harem.

houri Alluring, attractive.

three-tailed bashaw A Turkish pasha or ruler of high rank.

'pour me donner une contenance' In order to give me composure.

'Yes, bonny wee thing . . . I should tyne' From Robert Burns's poem 'The Bonny Wee Thing'.

The truest love that ever heart . . . A poem by Charlotte Brontë which echoes plot, theme, and action in *Jane Eyre*, thus showing her structural awareness.

suttee A Hindu custom by which a widow commits suicide on her husband's funeral pyre.

changeling A fairy-child exchanged by them for the parents' true child at birth.

I could not . . . see God for his creature: of whom I had made an idol Note that Jane regards this worship as sinful, and that she is punished for her sin when her idol proves to have feet of clay.

Chapter 25

Jane is uneasy and restless on the night before her wedding, largely because of what has happened on the preceding night.

She walks in the orchard and takes particular account of the split chestnut-tree. When she goes back to the library she gives further thought to the previous night – but Rochester arrives and she tells him what happened. At first she had had strange dreams, and later, when she awoke, it was to see a terrible woman in her room, placing the bridal veil on her head, and then tearing it apart. When she awoke she found the tattered veil. Rochester persuades her that the woman was Grace Poole, and tells her that when they have been married for a year and a day he will reveal the secret. Jane sleeps in Adèle's room with Adèle in her arms.

Commentary

Jane is very sensitive about her future name – 'Mrs Rochester' – almost as if she fears that she will never be Rochester's wife. The atmosphere is fraught with anticipation, and made dramatic by the mystery of what had happened the previous night, tension mounting because Jane does not immediately reveal what that was. The wind too seems to presage conflict or disaster, while the split chestnut-tree is, symbolically, the broken marriage to come and the later broken Rochester, whose roots prove to have remained intact. Jane's inward monologue unconsciously anticipates all that happens to Rochester later. Notice the tension aroused by the delay in Rochester's return, so that the reader shares Jane's fears that there may have been an accident. Jane's first dream is prophetic, with her consciousness of 'some barrier dividing us'. The child-dream, which previously presaged disaster or unhappiness for Jane, is here experienced again. It is prophetic of what happens to Thornfield and of the coming separation of Jane and Rochester, while the actuality of the woman in her room anticipates the revelation of the following day – 'it was not even that strange woman, Grace Poole'. The tearing of the veil of course prefigures the breaking of the marriage ceremony. There is a terrible irony when Rochester – who must be conscious of the risk he is taking – actually says to Jane, 'Is Thornfield Hall a ruin? Am I severed from you by insuperable obstacles?' Both are to be. In a strange, curious, and moving way, the chapter closes with Jane having a child in her arms, for the child of her dreams has become the reality of Adèle.

(D.V.) *Deo volente* God willing (Latin).

the trunk, split down the centre . . . The whole passage is rich in symbolism, and the paragraph beginning 'You did right to hold fast to each other' has a strong forecasting element and also links man and nature in a kind of unity – the storms destroy, the conflicts separate – in each case.

hypochondriac i.e. fear that something evil has happened.

blond White or black silk lace.

nothing remained but a shell-like wall A direct anticipation of the later fire.

transaction Happening, experience.

the veil, torn from top to bottom . . . Perhaps an unconscious Biblical echo – See Mark, xv, 38.

Revision questions on Chapters 21–25

1 Give an account of Jane's stay at Gateshead, bringing out clearly the main events.

2 Compare and contrast Georgiana and Eliza Reed.

3 Write an account of the events which lead to Jane's engagement to Rochester.

4 In what ways is Jane able to manage Rochester? Refer closely to the text in your answer.

5 In what ways does Charlotte Brontë maintain narrative tension in these chapters?

6 Write an essay on the part played by *either* (a) dreams *or* (b) nature and symbol in these chapters.

Chapter 26

Next day, the day of the wedding, Rochester appears anxious to get Jane to church quickly, and does so. Jane takes little account of anything before she reaches 'the grey old house of God' and the ceremony begins. This is dramatically interrupted by Mr Briggs, a solicitor, who declares that Rochester has a wife living. This is confirmed by Mr Mason, who declares that Rochester is married to his sister, Bertha Mason. Rochester eventually admits this, saying that he has taken good care that it shall not be known. He says that his wife has been mad for years. He takes the 'wedding' party back to Thornfield where he shows them the maniac, who is looked after by Grace Poole. This terrible scene is followed by Briggs revealing that Jane's uncle, now very ill, had received her letter announcing her approaching marriage to Mr Rochester. John Eyre had mentioned this to Mr Mason, who had of course realized that Rochester was contemplating bigamy. He had been persuaded to come to England to prevent this. Jane is overcome, and shuts herself away, offering up a prayer to God.

Commentary

The chapter depends on dramatic incident for its effects. Rochester's anxiety is shown in his restlessness to get the ceremony over with, even to the hurrying past Mrs Fairfax and the fact that there is hardly anybody at the wedding. On the way his 'Am I cruel in my love?' is to have immediate implications in the ensuing events. Dramatic tension rises with the almost casual mention of the 'two figures of strangers', and is heightened by Briggs's interruption and assertion. A superb image describes Rochester's reaction – 'His whole face was colourless rock'. The contrast between the physical power and presence of Rochester and the abject cowardice of Mason is stressed; Rochester's account is a passionately dramatic summary of his degradation through marriage. The spectacle of Bertha Mason is taut with violence, Rochester's wrestling with her shocking, ugly, yet when he compares her with Jane we are moved to compassion for what he has had to endure. We are aware of the morality of the situation – that Rochester was about to break the law. At the same time we are forced to question a law which chains a man to a beast. Jane's letter to Mr Eyre furthers the plot, and Jane's sufferings afterwards are tempered by her own qualities of courage in adversity.

fair or foul An echo of the first scene of *Macbeth* – 'Fair is foul and foul is fair', and I, 3 'So foul and fair a day'.
Marston Moor Site of the battle won by the Parliamentarians over King Charles I in 1644.
right about i.e. turn around.
ragout A dish made from highly seasoned meat.
Funchal An island in the same group as Madeira.
the first-born in the land of Egypt See Exodus xii, 29.

Chapter 27

Jane decides that she must leave Thornfield. When she comes out of her room she finds that Rochester is waiting for her. In the ensuing painful scene he reasons with her, says that he wants her to go away with him. He tells Jane the story of his marriage. It was his father's intention to leave all his fortune to his elder son, and it was therefore arranged that he, Edward Rochester, the younger son, should marry a West Indian heiress. He had been attracted by the girl's looks – he was very young – and had married her, only to discover quite soon afterwards that her mother and others of her family were mad. Bertha herself behaved unpredictably and violently and, within a short time, was also raving mad. Faced with the problem of his insane wife, he decided to bring her to England and to hide her at Thornfield. Despite her great feelings of love and pity for him, Jane will not yield to his entreaties that she should stay with him, refusing to become his mistress. That night she packs her few belongings and steals away from the house to the road, where she meets a coachman and persuades him to take her a long way off.

Commentary

This chapter marks the end of the second section of the novel, containing the moving aftermath of the marriage, Jane's decisive conduct, and the movement of the action away from Thornfield. Jane always listens to her inward voices, the voices of sanity and moral directive. The inward monologue becomes an inward dialogue which measures the emotional/moral struggle. That strength is balanced by physical weakness, since she has not eaten. Jane's capacity for forgiveness is generous, but again it is inward, and Rochester's suffering continues while Jane, in temporary weakness, wishes that she could die. Rochester's language is violent, Jane's replies, conditioned by her strong moral sense, firmly puritanical. Touching and kissing are forbidden. At the suggestion that she should become his mistress Jane summons her reserves of power – after a fit of weeping – for the suggestion is only oblique as far as Rochester is concerned – he does not really consider himself as married to Bertha Mason. As with his account of Céline Varens, Charlotte Brontë once again employs the retrospective technique to fill in the past, the past so essential to this part of the plot. The morality of that tale, which is both a moving and a degrading one, shows Rochester just as badly treated by his father and brother as Jane has been by Mrs Reed. The fact that his wife proves 'intemperate and unchaste' strengthens Rochester's plea, as does his account of his near suicide. The monologue is now used in Rochester's account of his motivation to return to Europe, with Hope personified to underline it. Here there is some structural unity with Jane's accounts of her inward debates. Rochester's arguments that he never meant to deceive, that he genuinely believed that he was not married, ring true, as does his rejection of debauchery in his own life. He is frank, too, about the mistresses he has kept, but it is a double-edged confession, for Jane judges – and probably rightly – that if she consented to be a mistress, she would be discarded too. His account of his watching Jane over the period of her time at Thornfield is imbued with tenderness and love. Jane's movement of compassion towards Rochester when she bends down to kiss him nearly undoes her resolve. The speed of the narrative matches the speed of Jane's departure; it is as if she must put distance between herself and Thornfield for fear that she will give in.

If the man who had but one little lamb . . See 2 Samuel, xii – this is where Nathan tells David the story of a poor man who had only one ewe lamb, his most treasured possession, which he was forced to kill.

this tent of Achan Achan hid part of the spoils of Jericho in his tent, ignoring God's command. When this was discovered he was killed. (Joshua, vii, 25).

upas-tree A tree which was reputed to be extremely poisonous and at one time believed to be destructive of all life around it.

mole-eyed i.e. blind.

cumbers Burdens.

Retreat Asylum.

St Petersburgh The present-day Leningrad.

gräfinnen Countesses (German).

antipodes Opposite.

Messalina's attribute Messalina was the sexually licentious wife of the Roman Emperor Claudius. The famous story about her tells of her spending the night in a number of brothels but still being unsatiated.

syncope i.e. failure of the heart, rendering the person unconscious or dead.

Chapter 28

Two days later Jane is set down by a signpost at Whitcross. She is in a North-Midland county, and she spends the night amid the heather on the moor. She is miserable, but prays that God will look after her. She also prays for Rochester. Next day, driven by hunger, she tries to get work and food, but few are willing to help her. Again she spends the night in the open, this time chilled to the bone by the cold and wet. She searches wearily the next day, calling at a parsonage and a farmhouse; at the latter she begs a thick slice of bread, and later some porridge at a cottage. Finally she comes to a house where she sees two young women and an elderly woman through the window. She is able to hear the conversation of Diana and Mary, the girls, the older woman being their servant, Hannah. She knocks at the door, which is opened by Hannah; the latter refuses to help her, but the man whom she is soon to know as St John Rivers is standing behind her, and takes her in to his sisters, seeing to it that they look after her.

Commentary

Jane's narrative embraces her need to be alone with 'the universal mother, Nature: I will seek her breast and ask repose'. The atmosphere of loneliness, particularly the fear of animals and poachers, is well conveyed. Jane, we note, always remembers her prayers, and her emotional sufferings are conveyed through physical imagery – gaping wounds, inward bleeding – while the familiar bird analogy is also used. Jane feels on the first night a widespread faith in God. The next day she realizes that her life must go on, the picture of the wagon convincing her that she must 'strive to live and bend to toil like the rest'. Jane's journey is a kind of pilgrim's progress, she is alternately rejected and accepted but without identity, forced to beg at last and still praying for direction. Jane's faith is justified; her prayer is answered, and there is a wonderfully graphic account of her viewing Diana and Mary, and of the considered stress on the Christian ethic of work. The device of Jane's being able to hear the conversation means that the speakers can be identified – it also promotes the plot sequence, for at the parsonage where she was rejected by the house-keeper we learned that the clergyman had gone to Marsh End because of the death of his father.

plained Complained.
knawn't Don't know.
mun Must.
these porridge i.e. with porridge being treated as a plural.
bombazeen Twill fabric composed of silk and worsted.
'"Da trat hervor . . ."' Then one stepped forward who was like a starry night to behold.
"Ich wage die Gedanken . . ." I weigh the thought in the balance of my anger, and the deeds with the passion of my fury.' Both quotations from *Die Rauber* (*The Robbers*) Act V, Scene 1. It was published in 1781.
ony Any.
Varry Very.
give ower Stop.
wor a'most stark Was almost dead.
wor mich i' your way Was very like you.
chimera Monster slain by Bellepheron (also, an incongruous idea).
agate Afoot.
mendicant Beggar.

Chapter 29

Jane is ill for some days. She overhears Diana and Mary talking about her sad and impoverished condition and also discussing her with St John. Eventually she gets up, goes downstairs, and finds out from Hannah about St John and his sisters. Jane castigates Hannah for being un-Christian enough to turn her away. When St John and his sisters return, Diana is particularly kind to Jane. Later she talks to them, tells them that she is without home and friends, but elaborates somewhat by saying that she is an orphan, was educated at Lowood, and that she is not to blame for her present position. She admits that she calls herself Jane Elliot, though that is not her real name; she is to stay with Diana and Mary, and St John will help her find work.

Commentary

Diana and Mary prove that they are genuine Christians, and Hannah proves that she has a heart. Jane's exhaustion is such that she can hardly dress herself. Despite this she has the strength to put Hannah in her place, though she also shows that her severity towards Hannah covers the true spirit of Christian forgiveness. Hannah's narrative is the means of providing Jane with both family and local information. Diana is warm and giving, Mary somewhat more reserved, St John extremely so, and distant with it. He is described in some detail, in particular his Greek profile resembling a statue. Jane detects 'elements within either restless, or hard, or eager'. His interrogation of Jane reveals his sharpness, his coldness, and his sense of justice. He is not an attractive character, except facially, for he virtually ignores Mary's discreet interruption. Notice Jane's remarkable self-possession in her account, with concealment, of how she came to leave Thornfield which, of course, she doesn't name. Jane nearly gives herself away when she is addressed as Miss Elliot. Jane is still determined to be independent, one of her salient characteristics, and St John is prepared 'coolly' to further this.

dunnut Do not.
brass Money.
kirstened Christened.
mun forgie Must forgive.
nor of mysel Than of myself.
like to look sharpish i.e. it's only right that I should be a bit sharp (alert).
wor wrang Was wrong.
raight down dacent little crater A thoroughly good little creature.
owd Old.
of a mak Of a type.
'threaped' Quarrelled.
even to licence i.e. even to an extreme.
solus Alone.

Chapter 30

Jane gets to like Diana and Mary, and reads as they read, even learning German from Diana, and in return showing her own talents in painting, talents which she uses to help the sisters with theirs. St John is always going on long excursions through the parish, and it is difficult for Jane to get to know him. She hears him preach, and is sure that his soul is not at peace. After about a month, Diana and Mary have to return to their posts as governesses in the south of England. This means that the house will be shut up. St John offers Jane the post of village schoolmistress in his parish of Moreton. He does not make it sound attractive. Just before Diana and Mary leave, a letter comes telling them that their uncle is dead. Instead of leaving them his large fortune, as had been expected, he has left it to one of their cousins.

Commentary

The emphasis is on the 'congeniality of tastes' which characterizes the relationship between Jane and the sisters. Jane responds, too, to nature around her – this again is one of her main traits – but her capacity for learning and instructing gives her positive fulfilment. There is a warmth about this relationship which is some compensation for what she has lost. There is too, I think, some adulation of Diana. St John is diagnosed by Jane as a man not at peace with himself; this is exemplified in the evenings when they sit together and she observes his inward tumult, the fact that he does not share their delight in nature, that his sermon has more doom and sternness in it than softness or warmth. Note a slight structural unity – Diana and Mary, here so independent, are in reality dependants like Jane, for they are governesses treated as Miss Ingram would have them treated. St John's address to Jane is pompous and cold – more like a ceremony or a sermon than an offer – and Jane shows that she is ready to do anything. St John continues to harangue her, but reveals his own restlessness. The letter announcing the uncle's death and the fact that there is no inheritance is a master-stroke of irony, and an important element in the plot which will reveal how Jane and her new friends are really cousins.

Calvinistic doctrines John Calvin (1509–64), who drew up one form
  of the Protestant religion, believed that a man's salvation depended on
  what God had determined for him before he was born.
that peace of God which passeth all understanding See Philippians iv, 7.
scathed Damaged.
cyphering i.e. arithmetic.

Revision questions on Chapters 26–30

1 Write an account of the most exciting incident in these chapters, bringing out clearly the elements which contribute to the excitement.

2 In what ways do you find yourself in sympathy with Rochester both before and after the wedding? Give reasons for your answer.

3 Analyse carefully Jane's feelings after the interruption of the wedding and before she leaves Thornfield.

4 Write character sketches of each of the Rivers family.

5 Write an account of Jane's character as it appears after she sets out from Thornfield until she accepts the post of schoolmistress in the village school.

Chapter 31

Jane settles in to the village school which has been opened by St John Rivers at Morton. She speculates on what might have been ('to have been now living in France, Mr Rochester's mistress'), and in the evening St John calls on her. They talk about Jane's experiences in the school, St John urges her to continue for some time at least, and then confides in her his own ambitions. He has decided that he wants to be a missionary, will be leaving Europe for the East but, as they are about to continue talking, the beautiful heiress Miss Oliver appears. She has come to enquire how Jane is getting on, but Jane realizes that Miss Oliver and St John are drawn to each other. Miss Oliver tries to persuade him to come home to see her father; St John refuses, obviously intent on his career rather than on her.

Commentary

The chapter shows Jane's capacity to adjust to new circumstances, though her attitude is one expressive of duty rather than sheer enjoyment of her work. She approaches the task with self-discipline, is scrupulously honest about what she finds wrong and what she objects to, and is convinced that she took the right decision in refusing to become Rochester's mistress. St John opens up, and this should give us a clue as to his interest in Jane, for he acknowledges that he would rather have been 'artist, author, orator, anything rather than that of a priest'. His determination to be a missionary smacks of obstinacy, as does his considered reaction to Rosamond Oliver. The latter is beautiful, direct, even petting Carlo and saying that he loves her (the dig is at St John's reserve), and talking freely to Jane without condescension, but with every indication that she will be of some help to her. With St John we get the effect of severe repression in refusing Rosamond Oliver, who is sensitive enough to put it down to the fact that his sisters have just left home.

'The air was mild, the dew was balm' From Scott's 'The Lay of the Last Minstrel' (1805).

Lot's Wife Genesis, xix, 26. She was said to have looked back at the destruction of Sodom and to have been turned into a pillar of salt as a consequence.

ken Sight.

Albion See note p.56.

Peri A fairy; in Persian lore, a superhuman being.

happy combination of the planets In modern terms, she was born under the right star-sign.

since the riots i.e. the Luddite Riots in Yorkshire in 1812. Their aim was to destroy the new machines which were causing unemployment.

hiatus Pause, gap.

Chapter 32

Jane gets on well with most of her pupils and becomes an accepted favourite in the village. Rosamond Oliver visits her regularly and praises Jane's pictures. This leads to her bringing her father to see Jane and as a result Jane is invited back to the Oliver home, and realizes that Mr Oliver would be quite happy for Rosamond and St John to marry. One holiday St John visits Jane in her cottage; he examines her drawing of Rosamond, Jane tells him that she knows of his feelings for her, and offers him the picture. She also advises him to 'take to yourself the original at once'. He refuses the portrait but admits his love for Rosamond, at the same time asserting that she would not make him a good wife. He appears to notice something written on a piece of paper Jane has been using, and hastily tears a slip from it.

Commentary

Jane learns much about her pupils and from them, and comes to an appreciation of them and their needs. She feels wanted – always she needs to feel this – and happy in her job, but her nightly dreams of Rochester and her awakenings from them to a passionate despair show just how deeply the current of her feelings runs. Rosamond is coquettish but not selfish; she times her visits so that she is virtually certain to see St John Rivers, and he manifests 'repressed fervour' at her coming. Jane defines her characteristics so that we get the impression of a grown-up Adèle – with beauty. She is vain and responds to Jane's drawing by wishing to be sketched herself. Jane subscribes to the work-ethic – she studies German on her holiday, and continues with Rosamond's portrait. Realizing that St John is something of a fanatic, she presses him towards the revelation of his feelings for Rosamond. In a sense she is officious, yet we feel with Jane that she adheres to the truth, and believes that the truth should always be revealed. She certainly embarrasses St John by her outspokenness. He is honest in return, and we respect his judgement of Rosamond – 'a sufferer, a labourer, a female apostle? Rosamond a missionary's wife? No!'. Unfortunately he responds to Jane's originality and independence, and we suspect that his last action in the chapter – which leaves us on the edge of mystery – has to do with this.

Amazon's Derived from the tribe of warrior-women in Greek mythology.
elysium The dwelling place of the blessed after death in Greek mythology.
bound Contain.
lusus naturae A freak of nature (Latin).
Schiller (1759–1805). The great German poet, dramatist, critic and historian.
Mammon The god of money, so named in the Bible and in Milton's *Paradise Lost*.
Marmion The poem by Sir Walter Scott, published in 1808, and thus indicating the period in which *Jane Eyre* is set.
the Cape i.e. the Cape of Good Hope.
'burst' . . . 'the silent sea' A quotation from Coleridge's 'The Rime of the Ancient Mariner', Part 2, lines 105–6 (1798).
That **is just as fixed as a rock . . .** This kind of image is used with different effect by Rochester. It is also reminiscent of the scene in one of Jane's paintings.
deistic philosophers These are the rationalist philosophers of the seventeenth and eighteenth centuries who held that God was wholly distinct from the physical universe. They founded their ideas largely on the teachings of Hobbes, Locke, Descartes and Newton.
"till this mortal shall put on immortality" See 1 Corinthians, xv, 53.
Cui bono? What's the use?
that caps the globe i.e. that beats everything.

Chapter 33

The next evening Jane is reading 'Marmion' when she is visited, despite the snow, by St John. He has been excited by what he saw on the piece of paper, the name Jane Eyre, but questions Jane about the school first. He tells her her own story as it had been written to him in a letter from Mr Briggs the solicitor, who has been searching for Jane to let her know that her uncle in Madeira has left her his fortune of £20,000. St John has realized that Jane is his own cousin, daughter of his mother's brother. Jane is amazed to hear about the money, but delighted to know that the Rivers family are her cousins. She insists upon sharing the fortune with St John and his sisters.

Commentary

The long arm of coincidence is certainly stretched in this chapter, with Jane finding her relations by chance after her journey, but not of course knowing them. We remark the scrupulous honesty of St John, but before he begins speaking Jane, bothered by his behaviour the previous day, considers that he may be suffering from 'a very cool and collected insanity'. He displays none of this in his narration, but rather a 'cold' pleasure in what he has to narrate. Jane reveals her own anxiety about Rochester, but is doomed to remain in ignorance, since St John neither knows nor cares about Rochester and is quite unswerving in his story and in his determination. Consequently while she hears the good news of her inheritance Jane is compelled to suffer in silence because of her anguish over what has become of Rochester. It is only Jane's strong powers of persuasion that influence St John to stay and complete the story of his relationship to her. Jane's delight in her found family can hardly be said to be shared by St John, who is as cold as ever. He is all for caution over the money; Jane is all impetuosity and generosity of spirit and pocket.

Day set on Norham's castled steep . . . From 'Marmion', with the omission of line 5 ('The loophole grates, where captives weep').
graved i.e. engraved, marked.
analogous Similar. Note the irony.
opiate Drug.
Medusa One of the three Gorgons in Greek mythology. Anyone who looked at her was turned to stone. Perseus killed her with his sword, using his shield as a mirror to avoid confronting her face-to-face.

Chapter 34

Jane closes the school for the Christmas holidays and goes with Hannah to prepare Moor House for the arrival of Mary and Diana. She tells St John that she intends to clean it down, and he replies that he will watch her carefully. She is very happy at Moor House for a while, bringing order out of chaos; on the evening when Diana and Mary are expected, St John arrives first. He is silent but Diana and Mary are joyful. A few days later St John tells them that Rosamond Oliver is to be married to a Mr Granby; he is quite 'serene' about it, but stays more at home with them. He begins to dominate Jane, asking her to give up German and to learn 'Hindostanee', which he is studying; she does so, and finds him an exacting master. One night Diana persuades St John to kiss Jane before she goes to bed. Jane meanwhile fails to get any replies to her letters to Mrs Fairfax. Through spring and into summer she works on, but one day at her studies breaks down before St John. Later he tells her that he is soon to go to India and tries, despite the fact that he expresses no love for her, to persuade Jane to marry him and to go with him as a fellow missionary. She agrees to go as his adopted sister but not as his wife. He treats this suggestion as impossible, and gives her a fortnight, while he is away, to reconsider the matter.

Commentary

Jane is intent on organizing and cleaning Moor House – for her, cleanliness is next to godliness. St John's restlessness is seen in his urging her to look beyond Moor House, though we later realize that he is moved by self-interest to say this. He cannot bring himself even to praise Jane's efforts in the house. Even when Diana and Mary arrive he seems unable to relax, yet duty in the shape of the boy's dying mother moves him at once. Diana and Mary are lively during Christmas, but St John as ever is withdrawn. It seems that he regards the marriage of Rosamond Oliver as something of a triumph for his will – 'You see, Jane, the battle is fought and the victory won.' But it is not so. The transference to Jane, without love, is accomplished in terms of selfishness. He needs a companion, he needs to rule, he needs to exact duty; Jane, trapped, writes for news of Rochester but, receiving none, goes into a decline, almost to the point of a breakdown. Since it is Jane, she does not break down but her resistance to St John is lowered by her depressed state. Yet she is rational in her appraisal of the marriage proposal, and her idea of going as St John's sister at once exposes the possessive and demanding nature of this cold and unswerving egoist. He has preached humility to Jane, but his own arrogance, his own spiritual and perhaps physical vanity, are affronted by Jane's proposal. To Jane there is more of death than life in his proposal, as she reveals in an explicit image when she says 'My iron shroud contracted round me'. Severity cannot do instead of warmth, distance cannot be a substitute for affection, the exercise of personal power cannot compel where there is no love. St John is obstinate, he cannot be crossed; the terrible irony is that what he wants is being done in the name of Christianity.

paysannes and Bäuerinnen Peasant women (French, German).

beau-ideal See note p.36.

confusion worse confounded A quotation from *Paradise Lost* Book II.

carte blanche Complete freedom.

Caffre African wilds.

meridian Height.

drawing away Dying.

Schiller See note p.70.

crabbed characters . . . i.e. cramped handwriting and elaborate figures.

him of Macedonia See Acts, xvi, 9 where Paul has the vision of the man of Macedonia who begs him to cross into that country and help the people there.

dust and ashes An echo of the funeral service, and another underlining of St John's unfortunate choice of words as far as Jane is concerned.

Demas See 2 Timothy, iv,10. He was one of the helpers of St Paul who deserted him.

My iron shroud . . . See the commentary above for the force of this image.

that frowning giant of a rock Note again the connection with one of Jane's paintings, and the symbolic associations with the firmness of Rochester and of her own love for him.

oblation The offering of the bread and wine of the Eucharist to God.

neophyte's . . . hierophant The latter is the priest who initiated the former into the secrets of the old Greek religion.

'Looked to river, looked to hill:' A quotation from Scott's 'The Lay of the Last Minstrel' (1805).

I would much rather he had knocked me down One understands why *Jane Eyre* made such an impact – no other nineteenth-century heroine (perhaps excluding Catherine Linton) would have uttered anything as unconventional and unladylike as this!

Chapter 35

St John does not go to Cambridge immediately, and Jane has a week of endurance in which he is hard and unforgiving to her. Jane tries to make friends with him before he goes, but he is firm and unyielding, and asks her if she is 'going to seek Mr Rochester'. Jane confides St John's proposal to Diana; that evening at supper she is greatly moved by his reading. She 'felt veneration for St John' and is on the point of agreeing to marry him there and then when she seems to hear the voice of Rochester calling her, and she breaks away. She prays, and waits for the daylight.

Commentary

Again we marvel at St John's fixity of purpose, his obstinate determination and the fundamental lack of humanity which causes him to subject Jane to his will. There is something pathetic in Diana's response to Jane's news, for there is little doubt that she would welcome the marriage, yet when Jane has told her the nature of the proposal she condemns the coldness, indeed unnaturalness of it, and obviously, silently, sides with Jane. The reading from the twenty-first chapter of Revelation is calculated to tell upon Jane's feelings – she is ever susceptible – but the mysterious voice, whether real or imagined, is a masterstroke of dramatic, even mystical narrative. Charlotte Brontë is reported to have said 'But it is a true thing; it really happened.' Be that as it may, it is the call of true love which kills off the pedantic but persuasive force of St John's arguments.

momently See note p.38.
ruth See note p.27.
seventy-and-seven times An echo of Matthew, xviii, 21–2.
the Society's aid i.e. The Society for Promoting Christian Knowledge.
'the night cometh when no man shall work' See John ix, 4.
the fate of Dives See the parable of Dives and Lazarus. Dives is the 'rich man' who was in torment after death when he saw the beggar Lazarus in Abraham's bosom (Luke xvi).

Revision questions on Chapters 31–35

1 Describe Jane's life at Morton and her work in the school.

2 Write an account of the interaction between St John Rivers and Rosamond Oliver. What does it tell us of each character?

3 Show how St John comes to discover the real identity of Jane.

4 Write a considered character sketch of St John as he appears in these chapters.

Chapter 36

Jane decides to return to Thornfield, and on the following day sets out on her long journey. When she arrives she discovers that the house is a blackened ruin. She learns from the landlord of the inn that after she had left Rochester had pensioned off Mrs Fairfax and sent Adèle away to school. Then, one night, his mad wife had set fire to the house; Rochester had attempted to rescue her from the battlements, but she had jumped to her death in the courtyard below. He had been badly injured by a falling beam and, as a result, had lost an eye and a hand. He is almost blind, and is living in seclusion in his other house at Ferndean. Jane immediately goes in search of him.

Commentary

Note once more that the series of journeys is increasingly important – this is the final journey in hope, if you like, contrasting with Jane's previous journey in despair. Jane's apprehension is conveyed by much self-questioning, but the narrative speed in a sense approximates to the time taken by the coach. Yet Jane's arrival, her first glimpse of the 'blackened ruin', is conveyed dramatically by way of descriptive contrast with an imaginary romantic lover coming upon his beloved. The reality is vivid too, characterized by 'the silence of death'. The reader, like Jane, is filled with apprehension until the landlord's story – and then Jane, for the second time in the novel, hears her own story again, or at least the part which encompassed her stay at Thornfield Hall. The movement of the narrative is swift and sure with tension.

Paul and Silas's prison They were imprisoned at Philippi because Paul restored a mad girl to sanity and thus incurred the anger of her masters; God sent an earthquake during the night so that they were released and the jailer was converted.

My heart leapt up An echo of Wordsworth's 'My heart leaps up when I behold/A rainbow in the sky'.
midge The word is emphatic of Jane's smallness.

Chapter 37

Jane eventually reaches Ferndean; intent on finding Rochester, she is able to watch him unseen. Presently she enters the house and, taking his tray of food from the servant Mary, she goes in to him and convinces him that she is real and that she has returned to him for good. After much interrogation from him about what she has been doing she promises to marry him. She learns that at the very time she had seemed to hear his voice, he had actually cried out to her and seemed to hear her voice in reply.

Commentary

It is noticeable that the day and the weather befit the sadness of what Jane is to see at Thornfield, and it is significant that Jane who, despite her independence, does not easily lose her consciousness of status, refers to Rochester as 'my master'. Notice that the image of the wild beast or bird is now used to characterize Rochester's state, whereas before it was definitive of Bertha Mason. Jane's ruse to see him shows both her ingenuity and her devotion, and the ensuing exchanges reflect her love and determination and his jealousy of her past, with particular reference to St John Rivers. Rochester is nothing if not passionate, and there is a terrible pathos as he strives to assert his strength, even in his adversity. Strikingly, Charlotte Brontë has him refer to the fact that he is 'no better than the old lightning-struck chestnut-tree in Thornfield orchard', a brilliant identification of reader and character, since we remember the incident symbolically and Rochester remembers it factually and symbolically and with the same associations. One other facet of Rochester's character is worthy of note – he has the humility (something we should not normally associate with him) to offer up his prayer of thanks to God for the restoration of Jane to him, and more particularly 'I humbly entreat my Redeemer to give me strength to lead henceforth a purer life than I have done hitherto'. Both Rochester and Jane testify to the maxim that adversity breeds a greater strength, a greater consciousness and sense of gratitude within the Christian framework.

game covers Shooting rights.
chaise Light, open horse-drawn carriage.
sightless Samson See note p.58.
only Lonely.
lameter Cripple.
"faux air" False appearance.
Nebuchadnezzar in the fields God punished Nebuchadnezzar for his pride and tyranny by depriving him of his reason for a time and forcing him to live like a beast in the fields (Daniel, iv, 33).
cicatrized Scarred.
brownie Good spirit.
changeling See note p.58.
If Saul could have had you for his David When Saul was tormented by an evil spirit, David helped him to recover his sanity by playing to him on the harp (1 Samuel, xvi, 23).
redd up Tidy.
royal eagle . . . sparrow The now familiar bird imagery to comment on the situation.
Jeune encore Still young.
a graceful Apollo . . . a Vulcan The god of light, poetry and music, and the god of fire respectively.
the valley of the shadow of death See Psalms, xxiii, 4.

Chapter 38

Jane and Rochester are married, and live happily ever after. Diana and Mary approve the match. St John does not answer the letter that Jane writes to him, though he corresponds with her later. When she completes her story, ten years after the marriage, she has received news that he is ill and soon to die. Diana marries a naval officer and Mary a clergyman, and both are happy. For the first two years after their marriage Rochester remains blind, but then slowly recovers the sight of his one eye. Jane is happy in the love of her husband and children.

Commentary

The opening sentence of the chapter – 'Reader, I married him' is definitive of the authorial control of narrative in *Jane Eyre*. It signals the happy ending after the adversities mentioned above. No place is given to the *real* wedding. It is typical of Jane that she puts herself out to see Adèle, and arranges – perhaps in the light of her own early school experiences – to have her sent to a more liberal establishment. Typical of the moral tone of the book too,

Adèle thus conditioned becomes a responsible and worthwhile person. The marriage is rather romantic wish-fulfilment, such phrases as 'we talk all day long' being rather cloying. But if this is romance there is an admirable balance of realism – St John, as we might expect, welcomes death. It is perhaps important that his are virtually the last words of the book exemplifying, as they do, a tenacity of faith. That faith, though with more warmth and tremulousness, was shared by Jane.

Revision questions on Chapters 36–38

1 Describe Jane's return to Thornfield.

2 In what ways does Charlotte Brontë maintain narrative tension in these chapters? You should refer closely to the text in your answer.

3 Describe in some detail Jane's being reunited with Rochester.

4 Do you find the last chapter of the novel satisfactory? Give reasons for your answer.

Charlotte Brontë's art in *Jane Eyre*
The characters

Jane Eyre

Portrait of a governess, disconnected, poor and plain.

The above quotation is by Jane about herself. She never treasures any illusions about what she looks like, and one is tempted to say that the child is mother of the woman, since Mrs Reed, Bessie and Miss Abbot all find her unattractive. It is Charlotte Brontë's great achievement that she makes the plain girl grow up into a plain woman without any attempt to romanticize her – she gives her an admirable consistency denied most heroines of fiction, who are generally gifted with good looks, either shyness or vivacity, and positive sex appeal in the presence of heroes or potential seducers. Jane is an unpropitious heroine, but she has a strength of character and independence, a curious mixture of faith and sensitivity and a sense of inferiority, a fine natural resilience and high moral integrity which compel our interest and often our admiration. She also has, from the outset, pride without vanity, and since her experiences and reactions span the whole length of the novel her characteristics will be given here 'in outline and no more'.

I have referred to Charlotte Brontë's consistency of presentation. Jane locked in the red room is recognizably the Jane condemned before the rest of the school after dropping her slate, the Jane almost turned away from the door by Hannah, the Jane who hears – or thinks she hears – Rochester's voice as she is about to succumb maritally to St John Rivers. She has a vivid imagination – witness her reaction to the loneliness of the red room and the fear that her uncle's ghost will manifest itself. Yet this sensitivity to atmosphere is balanced by courage and passion, for example, when she flies out at John Reed despite his size. The fact is that Jane's greatest need, and it virtually rules her life, is to be shown some love, and this of course, apart from the odd instance, is absent at Gateshead. Jane as child is superbly depicted, nowhere more so than in her first sight of Mr Brocklehurst, her small perspective perfectly conveying the height and the overpowering personality of that uncharitable clergyman. Jane, when she is not forced into an emotional or impulsive action, has a store of common sense which resists spiritual black-mail. For example, she answers Brocklehurst's question about what she should do to avoid Hell with the simple but practical expedient of 'I must keep in good health, and not die'. There is, as a famous comedian frequently observed, no answer to that.

When Jane expresses her deepest feelings she sometimes experiences exultation and 'the strangest sense of freedom'. Thus when she castigates Mrs Reed she frightens that woman so much that years later, when she is ill, she cannot get Jane out of her mind. Above all, in these early years Jane labours under a sense of injustice, largely on her own account but also, for example, on account of Helen Burns, particularly when the latter is punished by Miss Scatcherd. But Lowood unquestionably begins Jane's education, not just in the formal sense (and this is limited enough) but in the social, moral and spiritual senses as well. Miss Temple and Helen Burns are the prime influences, the first because of her obvious and selfless goodness and dedication, seen in her ordering the lunch of bread and cheese after the breakfast of burnt porridge, and also in her clearing Jane's name after Brocklehurst's public denunciation of her as a liar. This takes both courage and integrity. Helen Burns exercises a somewhat different influence, perhaps the more important of the two. From her Jane learns humility, to substitute rational thought for impulsiveness, to accept and endure without bitterness. The biographical tracings from Charlotte Brontë's younger sister are undoubtedly there, but they in no way militate against the realism in the portrayal of Helen. The scene where Miss Temple and Helen converse in front of Jane is seminal to Jane's subsequent development. It fires her with a kind of ambition, to love learning for learning's sake, and to love goodness and love wherever it is manifested. Lowood educates Jane for life, albeit limited life, but by the time she goes to Thornfield – and there is a long gap in the Lowood narrative which is passed over in a sentence – we notice a maturity of expression, a common-sense appraisal, a willingness to embrace experience and be receptive and, above all, a need to give and be accepted, and a need to love. It is not that Jane is ambitious; it is simply that she wants to experience 'A new place, in a new house, amongst new faces, under new circumstances'. The remarkable thing is that given the severe limitations of her life at Lowood she has the capacity to look outward and to brave the future.

Jane is accomplished by the standards of the time (her paintings should be closely examined, since they represent her subconscious fears as well as her conscious imagination), and when she re-meets Bessie the latter is moved to observe 'you will get on whether your relations notice you or not'. Arrived at Thornfield, Jane is receptive to the influence of the house, the kind gentility of Mrs Fairfax, the mystery of Grace Poole and the needs – and superficialities – of Adèle. But Jane's imagination is always reaching out towards new experience, and she soon realizes the limitations of Thornfield. Those limitations fortunately become somewhat irrelevant with the advent of Rochester, for although Jane has a sturdy independence of spirit which belies her frame, she also has – and this is far from the prototype women's-lib character some critics would have us believe she is – the need to serve, the need to be dependent on another's needs. Her first rescue of Rochester is symbolic of the other rescues of him which she carries out – the rescue from his past life, the attempted rescue from his present life through marriage, and the rescue of him when he is physically, mentally and emotionally scarred after the fire at Thornfield. She also of course rescues him practically from the first fire started by his mad wife, and, through the example of her integrity, from a potentially misguided liaison with Blanche Ingram. Here, however, we must remember that Rochester claims to have brought Blanche to Thornfield in order to inspire Jane's love through jealousy – sound psychology perhaps in view of Jane's temperament, though in fact he only succeeds in making her thoroughly miserable.

That first rescue – 'My help had been needed and claimed; I had given it' – brings Jane into direct interaction with Rochester. Inexperienced, she is yet able to cope with his abrupt, abrasive, unpredictable temperament because she has a core of commonsense and no airs and graces. Above all, she is transparently honest – witness her reply to Rochester's question as to whether he is handsome: 'No, sir.' Undesigning, she inspires confidences, and Rochester recognizes her unique qualities when he confides in her; Jane, who has little worldliness, displays a surprising tolerance over Rochester's past life and recognizes that she is falling in love with him, though it is doubtful whether she would use that phrase.

Jane is surprisingly practical – witness the fire – and has

reserves of stamina for one so small and slight – consider for
instance her sitting up with Mason *and* her journey to Whitcross
and the area around it. Just occasionally Jane can be devious,
though one must accept that her moral sense never deserts her.
To cross-question Grace Poole the night after the fire lacks
subtlety, though an oblique tribute is paid to Jane's honesty for
she is questioned herself in return. Of course she cannot know
that Grace is paid by Rochester to look after Bertha. But not
only does she question Grace Poole, she also questions herself –
with considerable self-deprecation – about the likelihood of her
having a place in Rochester's affections. She regards herself as a
'Poor stupid dupe!' but this does not diminish the strength of
her feelings. Those feelings are much to the fore with the
appearance of Blanche Ingram. The physical contrast and particularly the social awareness of Blanche Ingram affects Jane –
and she, naturally reserved, becomes more so. Yet such is her
capacity for experience that she enjoys the prospect of watching
these society people at play (and of watching Rochester's various
attitudes towards them), being particularly interested in the
charades, which seem to be loaded with references towards the
possible marriage of Rochester and Blanche Ingram.

Jane sees with the eye of love and the eye of truth as well, it
must be said, as with the eye of jealousy. For example, she sees
how superior Rochester is as *an individual* to his various affected
guests. She sees also that Blanche Ingram, for all her battery of
effects, fails to charm Rochester. And she sees, with just and
perceptive insight, the shallow nature of this society, its
indolence, its snobbery, its lack of the positive moral qualities
which she lives by. She comes through Rochester's test
unscathed because she is real. Inevitably Jane also suffers,
deluding herself that for financial and social reasons Rochester
will marry Blanche Ingram. There is a degree of masochism in
Jane, just as there is a degree of sadism in Rochester. In a sense
this makes the character of each fuller and more interesting; it
stops Jane from being too good, and it makes Rochester's suffering (over his marriage) all the more present to the reader.

Jane suffers from presentiments, as she calls them, and she is,
despite all her reasoning, essentially superstitious. Her
dreaming of a little child occurs twice in the novel, and the
second dream prefigures her return to see the woefully-ill Mrs
Reed. Here Jane evinces her genuine humanity – she would call

it Christianity – by putting duty before inclination. When she arrives at Gateshead she does all that she can for the dying woman who has treated her so badly in the past, but interestingly that imaginative verve which is both Jane's solace and her torture is released in her sketch of Rochester. It tells us where her heart is. When Mrs Reed tells Jane about her uncle's letter, it says much for Jane's maturity that she forgives her. In Jane's own words, 'I am passionate, but not vindictive'.

Such is Jane's rooted inferiority complex that when Rochester proposes to her she believes he is mocking her. This belief changes to delight, but still she is beset by presentiments, and these presentiments prove to be unequivocally true. Before that we note that Jane has the character to spurn the finery she is offered; she has no natural vanity, and would rather be herself, and not the clothes and jewellery with which Rochester would adorn her. She listens to Mrs Fairfax's warnings, and having balanced them in her own mind, she decides to keep Rochester at a distance. In view of her own feelings, this is a brave decision. Jane, ever uncertain, is greatly worried when Rochester returns late from a journey the day before the wedding; there are times when we feel that Jane is so vulnerable to thoughts and associations that she *knows* the wedding will not take place.

Jane's apprehensions are of course made worse by the appearance of Bertha Mason at her bedside, with the horrendous tearing of the veil symbolic of the coming wrecking of the marriage. The latter finds Jane bewildered by what she sees and hears. She retires to solitude almost broken – 'my life lorn, my love lost, my hope quenched, my faith death-struck' – but Jane's resilience, strength of character and *real* faith are never seen to better advantage than in this her worst adversity. She resists Rochester, though her suffering in doing so is as great as his; she overcomes physical weakness, even shows compassion for Rochester's wife ('she cannot help being mad') and finally decides to leave Thornfield. One has to admit that Jane is conventional in rejecting the offer of becoming Rochester's mistress, but we get the impression that she does so because (a) her principles would not let her accept this state and (b) because she intuitively feels that she would go the way of the other mistresses – that she would be discarded when her 'master' tired of her.

Jane's sufferings on and after her journey have been previously mentioned. Suffice to say that she displays fortitude and endurance in the physical, emotional and spiritual senses, and that we again note that quality of resilience which causes her to adapt successfully to new circumstances. Jane is a born survivor, dislikes having to conceal her real identity, is observant of Diana and Mary Rivers, helps whenever she can, notes St John and his austere practices, and even finds the stamina and intellectual impetus to study German and, later, Hindostanee. She is now living by bread and by faith and, although she longs for Rochester and tries to discover what has happened to him, she contrives to be useful, industrious, yet still retaining an independence of judgement. Jane is tidy and believes that her faith should be translated into practical action, as when she cleans through the Moor House and organizes the village school.

Her sensitivity, the loss of Rochester, a sense of frustration, all combine to undermine her when the obduracy of St John manifests itself in personal attachment to her. I say 'personal' only in the sense that St John sees how he can use her to further his essentially narrow aims and ambitions. The revelation of her inheritance enables Jane to be generous, to do what she most delights in doing – to give and to receive love and affection in return. She learns a deeper humility from her experiences in the village school, and even gets some pleasure from the fact that she becomes a favourite in the neighbourhood. But always in the background, and more often in the foreground now, is St John Rivers. Jane needs warmth and love; St John is cold and reserved. There is a deliberate irony in the presentation of Jane here. She rejects being Rochester's mistress; she rejects being St John's wife but, such is the spiritual blackmail that he is using upon her, that she comes to accept that marriage to him is God's will. At this stage, one is tempted to say at the highest moment of her neurosis, Jane hears – or thinks she hears – Rochester's voice. The fact is that her superstition and her imagination have coalesced to produce what she most wants – escape from St John, refuge and love with Rochester. The last part of the narrative is about just this. 'Reader, I married him' is the sum total of Jane's world. Of course she accepts the age difference between them, of course she accepts Rochester as maimed and reduced, and of course we are now in the world of romance after all the experiences of realism. Despite this, Jane Eyre remains a compelling character, profoundly sympathetic, her feelings and her consciousness thoroughly revealed and explored, convincing, immediate, felt. She is consistent in her actions and reactions, psychologically true in all situations. She epitomizes the realism and romance in all of us.

Edward Rochester

granite-hewn features . . . great, dark eyes . . . not without a certain change in their depths sometimes, which, if it was not softness, reminded you at least of that feeling.

Edward Rochester is one of the most vividly-drawn characters in English fiction. When he tells Jane his story after failing to marry her, he reveals that as a young man of twenty-two he had been sent to Jamaica by his 'avaricious, grasping' father to marry an heiress. Impulsive, generous and ignorant of the world, he allowed himself to be persuaded that he was in love with Bertha Mason. He married her knowing little of her character, and reaped the whirlwind of her debauched sensuality, a constitutional madness of the most degrading kind. In effect he is married to an animal. He contemplated suicide but drew back, and instead plunged into a life of superficial pleasure, going from mistress to mistress, occasionally jogged into moral responsibility as when, for example, he decides to take care of Adèle who may, or may not, be his child by Céline Varens. All this is retrospect, and all of it is told to Jane. It is almost as if he is unburdening himself, confessing and confiding because he has judged Jane's character and can measure her sympathy.

The Rochester we know is initially gruff, abrupt, a man of unpredictable needs. We must bear in mind throughout the narrative that his secret is his own and Grace Poole's; it is his decision to hide his wife at Thornfield while he travels Europe in the company of other women, returning home as to a prison, unable to move or even to converse freely. Jane has an immediate impact upon him – she inadvertently causes his accident, tends him, and thus prepares the way, unconsciously of course, for her own role in his life. She appeals to his imagination; she is in sharp contrast with anything he has known before. And just as she gives to him in that first incident, so she later saves his life in the fire, his integrity, by not marrying him, and his poor lopped life, by marrying him later. He refers to her as a fairy, sees her as a kind of sprite, questions her about her life at Lowood, remarks on her stamina, and comes to recognize the positive qualities which, one suspects, he has been sub-consciously searching for. But he is the master, she is the gover-ness, and it says much for Rochester's valuing true character as distinct from status that although he *appears* to condescend and *appears* to talk down to Jane he is not in fact doing so. He is testing her reactions and his own, making assurance doubly sure. It is Jane Rochester trusts in the crisis attendant upon Richard Mason's being wounded, for he knows that Jane is true.

But this impassioned man, strongly masculine, rather ugly though physically impressive at the same time, is capable of tenderness, courage, deceit (witness the near-bigamous mar-riage), anguish (when Jane refuses to stay with him after the break-up of his plans), a degree of fortitude in his adversity and some excusable degree of self-pity too. He is a man of strong emotions, not the least of which is jealousy; this is depicted with studied consistency, from his questioning of Jane implying that the girls at Lowood must have been in love with Brocklehurst, right through to his detailed interrogation of her on the subject of St John Rivers. Such is his insecurity, both with regard to his secret and with regard to Jane, that he sets up a house-party with the apparent intention of showing his attachment to Blanche Ingram and his impending marriage to her. He admits later to Jane that he intended to drive her mad with love for him out of jealousy; if this shows little concern for her feelings, it must be said that he shows great concern for her looks. This streak of sadism is part of Rochester's character, and it is seen at comic level when he disguises himself as a gipsy. This scene is one of the best in *Jane Eyre*, and it is not inconsistent, for we have already seen how Rochester can act – arguably, in view of his secret, his whole life is an act. There is little doubt that he takes great pleasure in misleading Blanche Ingram about his own financial state and in comparing her showy, snobbish, superficial behaviour with the quiet reserve but unquestionable integrity of Jane. As gipsy he reveals himself to Jane and he enjoys the joke, for it is an escape into fantasy from one terrible fact of life – his mad wife.

In seeking to 'marry' Jane, Rochester shows that he is selfish, yet just as Jane has the magnanimity of spirit to accept his past mistresses, so we accept the living degradation that Rochester endures. Rochester is the strong man of action – note the speed with which he sweeps Jane to the marriage service – the strong man reduced to physical prostration by Jane's firmness of decision. Yet we always feel sympathy for him, and he shows his consideration for Jane in a number of ways. For instance, at the end of the reunion scene, he stresses the age difference between them and emphasizes his physical wreckage. We remember Rochester's strength, and this makes his reduction all the more poignant. He is proud, highly intelligent, somewhat arrogant, characterized by swift transitions of mood and abrupt speeches, alternately teasing and serious, even witty. By a strange emphasis his ugliness is made to complement Jane's plainness, yet each of them is obviously a positive and compelling character, he is lovable despite his faults, indeed perhaps because of them. It is the secret of his great success as a character; brusque, volatile, warm, passionate, anguished, he is always articulate and never less than human.

St John Rivers

I had never seen that handsome featured face of his look more like chiselled marble than it did just now . . .

It seems natural to follow a résumé of Rochester's character with some focus on St John Rivers (*pron.* 'Sinjin'), who provides a direct contrast to him. In simple outline Rochester is ugly, St John perfectly formed, and where Rochester is warm St John is cold. Charlotte Brontë's genius consists in making the apparently unattractive man greatly appealing and compelling, while presenting the attractive man as virtuous, conscientious, driven by duty and ambition and thoroughly unlikeable. St John has what we should normally regard as heroic qualities, yet the fact is that he is an autocrat in a dog-collar. If Rochester represses his past by embracing the present both irresponsibly, as in his travels and mistresses, and warmly, as with Jane, St John represses natural feelings of love and attraction – for Rosamond Oliver – by a keen sense of vocation. He has an indomitable will that subdues all those human feelings he deems unfitting to his noble calling.

He reveals to Jane that when he first became a clergyman he was restless and longed for the satisfaction and excitement (and status) of a literary career, or of any career other than that of a priest where he might gain fame and reputation. But St John puts off the world, and he determines on complete denial and dedication by choosing to be a missionary. His pagan features –

'Greek face, a straight Classic nose; quite an Athenian mouth and chin' – belie a Christian fanaticism. If St John is capable of any enjoyment, and this is doubtful, he enjoys the prospect of martyrdom. Yet while all this is admirable, there is nothing lovable about it, for the first part of St John's creed must involve sacrificing others to his feelings and his needs. Everything subserves his consuming purpose. His attitude towards Rosamond Oliver's love – and he certainly does not consider her feelings – is for him 'a last conflict with human weakness . . . I know I shall overcome, because I have vowed that I *will* overcome'. He exults in the triumph when he does, though we know from his conversations with Jane that he has endured great suffering in doing so.

But it is in St John's relations with Jane that we feel strongly the limitations and the positive, dangerous, wilful behaviour of the fanatic. Rosamond is not a suitable helpmeet for him in his chosen life's work; Jane, with her special sense of duty (and duty is uppermost in St John's mind) is. He plays on that sense, and on Jane's need to give herself, without thought of her as an individual, with no concept of the deep feelings she possesses. He does not foresee that if Jane were to accompany him to India she might fall in love with him. She sees this danger, and says to Diana: 'In that case my lot would become unspeakably wretched. He would not want me to love him; and if I showed the feeling, he would make me sensible that it was a superfluity, unrequited by him, unbecoming in me.' He sees Jane as a work-object, 'a conductress of Indian schools', yet when she has the temerity to suggest to him that she accompany him as his sister he rejects it – his pride and the practical nature of what *he* has conceived, plus the fact that his will has been crossed, determine him on the course of moral and spiritual blackmail which he now conducts against her. He is hard and cruel, since his devotion to his religion means the rejection of all that is humanly sympathetic and warm. In fact he persecutes Jane in order to bend her to his will, prays in the name but not the spirit of religion that she will be forced to change her mind, and nearly has his prayer answered. It is only thwarted by the voice, real or imagined, of Rochester in Jane's consciousness; the reader feels with agonizing relief that in any case it is the voice of sanity.

Yet St John is kind to his sisters, scrupulous in his conduct, letting Jane know that she is an heiress, and is most unwilling that she should divide her fortune, though he appreciates the justice of her action. He does what he wants to do, and sees what he wants to see. When Jane writes to give him the news of her marriage to Mr Rochester he ignores it, but he keeps up a regular correspondence with her afterwards, hoping that she is happy and that she does not live without God. In the structure of the novel he has virtually the last word, for while Jane enjoys the happiness of life St John moves inexorably, wishfully, towards death, and Jane knows that she will soon hear 'that the good and faithful servant has been called at length into the joy of his Lord'.

St John Rivers is a remarkable character. Whenever he speaks, even in kindness, as when he first gives Jane shelter, we are aware of a kind of severity, an inability to translate goodness into sympathetic and intimate relationships. For him Good is God, duty is absolute, dedication the first ideal of service. He is narrow, rigorous, a brilliant psychological study of the kind of man who is able to subdue the temptations of the flesh and who, as a result, loses what humanity he had in the need to devote himself exclusively to what he sees as his faith. I have said 'what he sees' deliberately; for what he sees is not Christianity, it is the terrible illusion of certainty, the certainty of being exclusively, practically, dogmatically right. St John, lacking humility and the fundamental which we call Christian charity, undoubtedly does good; and perhaps it is because he has been so successful in ridding himself of human feelings that a disinterested service dictated by duty is the permanent substitute for living.

Mrs Reed

she shook me most soundly, she boxed both my ears,
and then left me without a word.

Mrs Reed could so easily fall into the cruel-aunt stereotype found in many novels and it is a tribute to Charlotte Brontë's characterization that she does not. Mrs Reed comes across as a person with motives and actions so convincing that the reader is able to believe in her as a real woman beset (a) by children who she indulges all the time and (b) by guilt because of her treatment of Jane and the latter's justified rebellion against her. She had disliked Jane's mother heartily, as we learn, partly because of her husband's affection for his sister, and partly because he had supported Mrs Eyre against the rest of the family when she married a penniless clergyman, Jane's father. From the first, therefore, she had objected to her husband's plan to bring into their home the soon-orphaned daughter of this ill-fated match, and detested the 'sickly, whining, pining thing'. She disliked too the fact that her husband paid considerable attention to Jane and his desire to make his own children friendly to the 'little beggar'; most of all she resented his anger when they showed their own dislike for their little cousin.

Mrs Reed was compelled, most reluctantly, to promise her husband on his death-bed that she would keep the child, and although she kept the promise, she does so with the minimum amount of commitment to her husband's generous and charitable feelings. She soon developed an antipathy to the quiet, studious and plain child, always putting her own children first and never giving Jane any love. When she sends Jane to the red room she shows that she has no understanding of the terrors that can assail an imaginative and lonely child; temporarily frightened by the force of Jane's fit in the red room, she falls back on her accusations that Jane was a liar who needed punishment. She conveniently seizes upon Mr Lloyd's suggestion that Jane should go to school, deliberately damns Jane in front of Mr Brocklehurst, and hates her all the more when Jane bursts out against her, probably because she recognizes the truth of what Jane is saying. She is seen to be unscrupulous – though later her conscience will trouble her – when she replies to Jane's uncle in Madeira that Jane has died during the fever outbreak at Lowood. That evil deed haunts her, the way she has indulged her own children rebounds back upon her, and, her mind unhinged by her own illness and by the suicide of her son, she sends for Jane in order to confess her crime. Yet, when Jane arrives, her confession has nothing of true repentance in it; it is more the *need* to confess which she feels will bring absolution from her feelings, but her dislike for her niece is as strong as ever. She actually blames Jane for her very existence, and with her dying breath declares: 'You were born, I think, to be my torment: my last hour is racked by the recollection of a deed which, but for you, I should never have been tempted to commit.' Selfish, indulgent, blind alike to right behaviour, compassion, warmth and justice, Mrs Reed represents a convincing portrait of character in unkind action. Though Jane is sympathetic and gives to her in her hour of need, Mrs Reed never escapes from the narrow degrading confines of self.

Eliza and Georgiana Reed

very thin too, with a sallow face and severe mien . . .
a full-blown, very plump damsel, fair as waxwork.

These are minor characters in the novel, but they clearly represent two distinctive types of womanhood, and as children they are carefully drawn to show their particular traits. For example, Eliza as a child is a greedy and scheming little creature, her interest in money so strong that, according to Jane, she would have sold the hair off her head for profit. At first she hoards the money she obtains from selling the produce of her little garden to her mother's gardener, but when one of the places where she hides her money is discovered, she 'lends' it to her mother at an exorbitant rate of interest.

When Jane meets Eliza again at the time of Mrs Reed's death, there is a considerable change in her character, further evidence of Charlotte's focus on *developing* her characters. She has now become somewhat nun-like in appearance and is attached to the church. Much of her time is spent in reading the Rubric and in stitching an altar cloth; she attends church three times on Sunday, as well as going to every weekday service, regardless of the weather. Though generally not given to much conversation, she is annoyed by Georgiana's complaints about the dullness of the house and delivers a tirade upon her sister's uselessness, further declaring that she will have nothing to do with Georgiana after their mother's death.

There is every evidence that Eliza is a woman of very strong will since, according to Bessie and Georgiana, she has prevented the latter's marriage to Lord Edwin Vere. She could not bear to see her sister raised above herself in rank. She shows little pity for her mother, who lies helpless, and her only comment when Mrs Reed dies is: 'With her constitution she should have lived to a good old age; her life was shortened by trouble.' Yet we feel that Eliza has determinedly repressed what feelings she has in the interests of a rather arid religious dedication (compare her with St John Rivers in this respect), for when her mother finally dies 'a spasm constricted her mouth for an instant', though she is unable to shed tears. She retires to a nunnery, takes the veil after studying the Roman Catholic religion, and later becomes Mother Superior of her convent. Georgiana refers to her as selfish and heartless, and there is some truth in the accusation; certainly she lacks warmth and sympathy, and there is an irony in Charlotte's presentation, for this religious woman lacks the fundamental warmth of practical Christianity. There is little doubt, though, that she is seen in reaction against the superficial life of her mother, brother and sister, and that this reaction takes the extreme form of denial of the world.

Georgiana as child is vain, greedy, having the looks the servants adore and a complementary autocratic self-indulgence — she orders Jane not to interfere with her playthings when Jane is in fact merely tidying the dolls' house. In adulthood she has become voluptuous, always playing the coquette, with 'languishing blue eyes and ringleted yellow hair'. Although she is apparently weak, she is also hard and obstinate. She is a fashionable young lady who has just enjoyed a season in town, and has only just missed making a most advantageous marriage because of the jealousy of her sister. At first Georgiana condescends to Jane who is, after all, only a governess and wears unfashionable clothes, but when she finds that her cousin can sketch she becomes more friendly, and insists that Jane contributes a watercolour to her album. She then confides in Jane, who has to hear all about the winter in town. Georgiana's indolence is a great contrast to Eliza's industry but, like Eliza, she shows little feeling for her mother, even wishing that she could 'get out of the way for a month or two, till all was over'. When her mother dies, she weeps loudly and says that she cannot go into the room where her mother is lying. Jane is disgusted with her 'feeble-minded wailings', but Georgiana survives to make the advantageous match that she wanted though, ironically, it is with a 'wealthy, worn-out man of fashion'.

John Reed

He bullied and punished me . . . continually.

Although he plays but little part in the action, this most repulsive of the Reed children is fourteen years old when the story opens. Spoiled and indulged in his moral and physical criminality by his mother (she even interrupts his education for a month or two 'on account of his delicate health') he takes a great delight in tormenting Jane. Like all bullies he is a coward, flying to his mother in complaint when she dares to hit back. He gorges himself with food, and makes himself bilious. Thereafter we only hear of him through Bessie. When the latter visits Jane just before she leaves for Thornfield, she tells Jane that it is intended that John shall be a barrister; but he is so dissipated that he has failed an examination. This is the pattern of his future life. When Robert comes to Thornfield to ask Jane to visit Mrs Reed in her final illness, he brings news that John had ruined his health and lost his money by associating with worthless men and women. He had tried to persuade his mother to give up her house and fortune to him and had committed suicide when she refused. As she is dying Mrs Reed rambles on about her worthless son, excusing him by saying that although he gambles dreadfully, he is beset by sharpers. Spoilt and indulged in childhood, John Reed had little chance in adulthood of recovering from a system of self-indulgence which mars and scars character and morality for life.

Bessie Lee

Poor Miss Jane is to be pitied, too, Abbot.

Bessie first shows affection for the orphaned Jane after the incident in the red room when Jane becomes ill. At this time Bessie is a slim girl 'with black hair, dark eyes, very nice features and a good clear complexion'. Naturally she follows her mistress in her attitude towards Jane, and treats the child as an inferior to her cousins; perhaps she genuinely believes this to be so, for she obviously admires the beautiful Georgiana. But her patience is tried by the Reed children, and some of her frustration is vented on Jane. She has a 'remarkable knack of narrative', Jane tells us, and delights the children with her songs and nursery rhymes. When Jane is ill, Bessie is kind and gentle towards her. When Jane is kept in the nursery while Eliza and Georgiana go down to meet their mother's guests, Bessie sometimes tucks her up and kisses her, though she does not stay, preferring to pass her evenings with the lively company in the kitchen. She is puzzled by Jane's solitary habits, and tries to persuade her to be less shy and frightened; when she comes to say goodbye to her she is surprised to find that she is 'fonder of you than of all the others'. When Jane meets Bessie again after her eight years at Lowood, it is quite obvious (a) that Bessie has a sincere affection for Jane and (b) that she has spent some time defending Jane and praising her potential abilities, now translated into fact in Jane's playing the piano well and drawing too. She shows her concern for Jane by giving her the news of her uncle Mr Eyre visiting Gateshead in search of her. When Jane herself returns to Gateshead to see her dying aunt she finds Bessie in an attractive lodge with white curtains, spotless floor and burnished grate, with her family playing around her. There is little doubt that Bessie's character derives in part from that of Tabby (Tabitha Aykroyd), the faithful servant to the Brontë family, though Tabby was much older than Bessie when she first came to the Brontë home at Haworth.

Mr Brocklehurst

The black marble clergyman.

One must resist the biographical associations with the Reverend Carus Wilson who founded the Cowan Bridge School, and concentrate on Brocklehurst as he appears in the fictional account of Lowood. As seen through the eyes of the child Jane Eyre he is an ogre with scarcely a redeeming feature. When she first meets him he appears to her like a black pillar with a grim face 'like a carved mask, placed above the shaft by way of capital'. When he stoops to speak to her he appears to have the same characteristics as the wolf appeared to have to Red Riding Hood in the nursery story. He is pompous, pedantic, self-congratulatory, his conversation terrifying with its mention of death and naughty children. He obviously exacts from children the answers he wants to fit them for heaven, though his own unfitness for salvation never occurs to him. He is the complete hypocrite who enjoys bullying the little girl who is falsely stigmatized as a liar, preaching not charity or humility but the stern doctrine of unthinking obedience. What he prescribes for the girls at Lowood he manifestly does not apply to his own daughters, whose topknots are certainly curled and who dress in a very expensive fashion. When Jane accidentally drops her slate, Brocklehurst exacts the utmost morality and religiosity from the situation. He has Jane placed upon a stool before the whole school and condemned as a liar. It does not suit him to enquire into the justice or otherwise of the accusation, for naturally he accepts the word of Jane's 'benefactress'. He can hardly be called sadistic, since he has no feelings in his public office which involve anything but rigid discipline to be imposed on the girls 'to render them hardy, patient, self-denying'. He is mean, looking closely and pettily to the economics of Lowood, cruel, as when he orders the topknots to be cut off, ignorant, foolish and unconsciously humorous (witness his refusal to recognize that some hair curls naturally), dogmatic, insensitive, autocratic. When typhus comes to Lowood he is of course conspicuous by his absence and, although mortified by what is said about him – he is after all largely responsible for what has occurred – he does not resign his position. Since he is too wealthy to be turned away he retains his position as treasurer, though others see that the school is improved. 'His office of inspector was shared by those who knew how to combine reason with strictness, comfort with economy, compassion with uprightness.' These qualities are outside Mr Brocklehurst's character, outside the dogma of inverted Christianity by which he lives.

Miss Temple

'Don't be afraid, Jane, I saw it was an accident;
you shall not be punished.'

The superintendent of Lowood Institution stands in total contrast to Mr Brocklehurst. She is a true Christian, practising Christian principles in her daily life, warm, sympathetic, just, kind and cultured. It is obvious that she is drawn with loving care, and she appears to derive from a real-life person. The first instance of the concern and width of Miss Temple's compassion is when Jane arrives after her long and unaccompanied journey from Gateshead. Miss Temple expresses surprise that such a young child has been sent alone, and deals very gently with her. She is plainly dressed always as befits her station, and she has a 'stately air and carriage' which catches Jane's attention. She is dignified, well-controlled, and for the most part serene, facing up to situations as they occur; she is capable of decision, as we see when, after the disgusting breakfast of burnt porridge, she gives orders for the bread and cheese lunch to be served to the girls. She is prepared to endure Brocklehurst's reprimand, and cannot quite contain her humour when Mr Brocklehurst comments on Julia Severn's hair. She is almost a kind of Florence

Nightingale before her time during the typhus outbreak, and she has a stoic – but not cold – attitude towards the pettinesses of life, as when the housekeeper refuses to send up any extra bread and butter when she is entertaining Helen Burns and Jane. Her sense of justice is always in evidence, and as Mr Brocklehurst goes through his list of complaints, she manages to defend her pupils rather than her own actions from his strictures. She is particularly just to Jane, sending away to Mr Lloyd to corroborate Jane's story, and then vindicating the child before the whole school. She is both kind and clever, and individually as well as communally compassionate, as she shows both Jane and Helen. If she is somewhat idealized through her goodness, she is never cloying, and there is little doubt that she is Jane's model in action and in spiritual and moral attitudes. When she leaves Lowood, part of Jane's reason for staying is gone. Her quiet but effective control, the cultural ethos she promotes, and above all the kindness and concern of her daily life with her pupils, all testify to a sincere, dedicated and thoroughly sympathetic woman.

Helen Burns

She neither wept nor blushed.

It is always assumed that Helen Burns derives from Charlotte's eldest sister, Maria, whom Mrs Gaskell wrote of as being 'far superior in mind to any of her playfellows and companions', adding 'I need hardly say that Helen Burns is as exact a transcript of Maria Brontë as Charlotte's wonderful power of reproducing character could give'. Certainly Helen is thoroughly convincing, and she is convincing in the same way as Rochester is. She is far from perfect and, because of this, she is not a stereotype. Charlotte herself claimed 'I have exaggerated nothing there'. The first thing that strikes the reader about Helen Burns is her individuality, seen initially in the precocity which finds her reading Dr Johnson's *Rasselas*, an unusual choice for a girl of thirteen. She answers Jane's questions patiently, but she returns to the private world of her reading as soon as she can. She obviously has a brilliant mind, though she does not give herself fully to practical and everyday things, and thus comes in for a fair amount of punishment. She is naturally studious and certainly quick, and there is every evidence that she has read as widely as she can. On the evening when Miss Temple entertains Jane and Helen to tea, she talks to Miss Temple about French and English authors, and finally construes some Virgil. She is very kind to Jane, particularly after Brocklehurst's inflammatory visit, when she gives the younger girl some excellent and surprisingly mature advice: 'If all the world hated you, and believed you wicked, while your own conscience approved you, and absolved you from guilt, you would not be without friends.' It shows a moral and spiritual responsibility which communicates itself to Jane and which influences the future course of her life. In fact, it would be true to say that, Miss Temple apart, Helen is the major influence on Jane, and that her independence, her faith, her strong moral sense of right and wrong, all these condition the young Jane into being the woman of integrity which she assuredly becomes.

Jane feels greatly indignant on Helen's behalf, yet Helen has the self-honesty to admit her faults, like those of untidiness or inattentiveness. For these she is punished severely, particularly by Miss Scatcherd. Yet Helen refuses to blame her persecutor; she has a keen sense of fairness for such a young child, a maturity of perspective which causes her to excuse her tormentor on the grounds that 'life appears to me too short to be spent in nursing animosity or registering wrongs'. She has a stoic attitude towards suffering and the endurance of wrongs, advising Jane to forget the cruelty of Mrs Reed, just as she is able to put away the cruelty of Miss Scatcherd. Allied to this stoic fortitude is her deep religious feeling, and she also has that rare capacity for withdrawing into herself, something which the Brontës shared. We remember Helen being sent out of the history lesson on Jane's first afternoon at Lowood. Jane, who of course hardly knows her then, expects her to show signs of distress. She doesn't, for Helen's faith causes her to look beyond the petty present into the visionary future, 'beyond her situation; of something not round her nor before her'. But as well as being a reality Helen is also a symbol – of courage, of compassion, of faith, of fortitude.

Mrs Fairfax

A model of elderly English respectability.

Jane has her own incorrect picture of Mrs Fairfax – whom she thinks is the owner of Thornfield, not the housekeeper   before she arrives at the house. Whereas she thought she might be frigid and uncivil, she finds that Mrs Fairfax is not someone to be feared, though she is to be respected. Jane is reassured by first seeing Mrs Fairfax knitting before a cheerful fire in the snug little room at Thornfield, with her cat by her side. She treats Jane like a visitor – the prospect of such companionship will relieve her own sense of loneliness at times – and not like a servant, and this shows her inherent kindness and good breeding. She is curious about Adèle but considerate towards her. She has a natural sense of her own status, for although she is related to Rochester (her late husband, a clergyman, was second cousin to Rochester's mother) she does not 'presume on the connexion'. She is unassuming in her attitude towards her employer and his guests. Though she is quiet she finds Thornfield dull and boring, and sees that Jane will relieve the monotony. Her loneliness is now almost over, and she will not again have to depend on the maid Leah to read to her. I have mentioned her sense of status, which is not an inflated one, but I must also refer to the fact that she is a good and responsible housekeeper; she respects the conventions and the gradations of position, her behaviour to the servants conditioned by the fact that 'they are only servants and one can't converse with them on terms of equality; one must keep them at due distance for fear of losing one's authority'.

It must be acknowledged that Mrs Fairfax is limited, and it is doubtful whether she has a sense of humour. She cannot understand Rochester's teasing of Jane, particularly in the 'men in green' sequence, and when on Midsummer's Eve Jane and Rochester enter the house very late she is shocked, treating Jane with considerable coolness the next morning. She cannot believe that Rochester is engaged to Jane, though she tries somewhat pathetically to adapt herself to this new idea. Her instinct is to offer her congratulations, but these die away on her lips as she looks into Jane's face and tries to see what it is that has attracted Rochester to her. She is frankly sceptical about the success of the marriage, and warns Jane to keep Rochester at a distance during the period of their courtship, something which Jane certainly succeeds in doing. It is obvious that she does not know that Rochester is already married, for we can't believe that she would allow Jane to be deceived, though she does know of the mad-woman's presence in the house, for she tells Grace Poole to

'Remember directions!'. Rochester himself confirms her ignorance of what was going on later in the words 'Mrs Fairfax may indeed have suspected something, but she could have gained no precise knowledge as to facts'. Before the wedding she begins to appreciate Jane's control over Rochester, and we feel that she may have been thinking more of Jane's position in the relationship than of Rochester's. She is a good religious woman who reads her Bible every day, and she is kind-hearted and conventional. Indeed so much so that she is almost incapable of shifting her position to take in any new ideas or, more particularly, to accept any change.

Adèle Varens

My pupil was a lively child who had been spoilt and indulged, and therefore was sometimes wayward.

Adèle is the illegitimate child of Céline Varens, the opera-dancer who had been Rochester's mistress, and in some ways she has inherited what seem to have been her mother's characteristics – she is superficial, delights in dress and in receiving presents, is silly, anxious to please (in view of her removal from her mother, perhaps this is sound child psychology on Charlotte's part) though she has amazing self-possession for one so young. She craves from Rochester's house-party guests the attention she has been accustomed to receive from her mother's admirers. Yet despite all this – it is the nurture of her education which has to fight the characteristics she has inherited – there is something attractive and pathetic about her. We warm to the fact that she gets on Blanche Ingram's nerves – can it be that that young lady cannot bear to think of Rochester having a mistress in the past? – and we also feel sorry for her when she craves to go with Rochester and Jane on their shopping expedition before their marriage. She shows her sense of rightness when she asks if Rochester has bought a present for Jane as well as her, and although she is not very bright at her lessons Jane finds her docile and teachable enough for the most part. But when Adèle is excited her natural vivacity makes her swift to respond both mentally and physically. Despite the superficiality already referred to she is warm-hearted and, in her impulsive way, becomes very fond of Jane, and we notice that Jane is responsible for altering her school and making sure that she gets on better; the result is that Adèle in adulthood repays all the kindness that Jane has shown her, visits her family and is a good and worth-while person.

Grace Poole

a set, square-made figure, red-haired, and with a hard, plain face.

We see little of Grace Poole, who is the well-paid nurse employed by Rochester to look after his mad wife. She is in almost constant attendance upon the dreadful creature in the upper room at Thornfield, spending one hour a day with the other servants, when she goes down to the kitchen to have her dinner and 'to smoke a moderate pipe'. Jane once hears Leah and the charwoman discussing Mrs Poole and declaring that although her wages are five times as much as Leah's she fully earns them. She puts away a regular proportion of her wages, and, because of the nature of her surveillance, turns to drink; when she does this her charge sometimes manages to escape. Grace is on one occasion interrogated by Jane, but she remains cool under questioning and turns the tables on Jane by questioning her. Jane of course is deceived into thinking that it is Grace's laugh and that the actions are Grace's actions too. Such is the narrative skill that the reader, on the first reading of the novel, feels the same as Jane.

Blanche Ingram

A strapper — a real strapper, Jane: big, brown and buxom.

There would be little point in examining all the house-guests brought by Rochester to Thornfield, though it is almost true to say that they are seen ironically and satirically, with Charlotte via Jane showing an acute sense of class. Since Blanche is apparently the focus of Rochester's interest she becomes the focus of ours. It would be true to say that she is a thoroughly obnoxious person. Charlotte apparently drew on her experience in her first employment, describing the society guests there present as being 'proud as peacocks'. Blanche and her mother talk in the stilted language of affectation and aristocratic status — 'Am I right, Baroness Ingram of Ingram Park?' asks Blanche, and her mother replies, almost on superior cue, 'My lily flower, you are right, as always.' Now in a sense this is absurdity, and I think we must concede that Charlotte is either writing the language of *parody* or she is simply being *satirical* about affectation and snobbery. The result is caricature; Blanche shows the insolent self-assurance of the girl who possesses wealth and beauty. Her arrogance is built-in, extending not only to her speech but to the way she carries herself. She is a beautiful girl, conscious at all times of her rank; she is 'moulded like a Diana' but has a 'low brow' and 'high features'. Like the Reed children, she has been thoroughly spoilt, and because of her own nature and the indulgence of an adoring and ambitious mother, she is completely selfish and unscrupulous. She appears to have made up her mind to marry Rochester, in the first instance because of his fortune and position, and in the second because he is one of the few eligible bachelors in her narrow circle. She is now twenty-four years old and needs to marry, since it is six years since she 'came out'; she is accomplished, her piano-playing is brilliant, her singing very fine, and she speaks French 'with fluency and a good accent'. She looks down on the governess and retails jokes about her own teasing and provocative treatment of such menials in her own family, though she does appear to sense some threat from Jane. The account she gives of how she and her brother persecuted their poor Miss Wilson who dared to fall in love with the tutor is an index to the nature of their characters – mean, sadistic, un-moral, arrogant. Doubtless she wishes to make Jane feel uncomfortable and to increase her sense of insecurity and uncertainty. When Jane comes to ask Rochester if she can go to see Mrs Reed, Blanche's superiority is advanced to the full – 'Does that person want you?' she asks him, looking at Jane haughtily as if to demand 'What can the creeping creature want now?' And finally one must add to this catalogue of Blanche's faults the cardinal one of mercenariness. Duped by the 'gipsy' into believing that Rochester is not rich, she goes into a sulk, and it is pretty obvious why the house-party is broken up shortly afterwards. Rochester calls her a 'strapper', and although he is intentionally drawing her physical contrast with Jane there is a shade of disrespect about the term. She is 'big' in status but not in heart or moral substance.

Bertha Rochester

The clothed hyena.

Charlotte Brontë wrote of Rochester's wife in one of her letters, 'I agree that the character is shocking, but I know it is but too natural.

There is a phase of insanity which may be called moral madness, where all that is good or even human seems to disappear from the mind and a fiend nature replaces it.' Apart from our glimpses and the head-on look immediately after the broken marriage ceremony, all that is said of Bertha is reported. Inheriting the streak of insanity in the family she becomes progressively worse after the marriage, Rochester finding her mind 'coarse and perverse' and her temper 'violent and unreasonable'. There is then a rapid deterioration; Bertha becomes 'intemperate and unchaste', Rochester describes the various other manifestations which bring him close to suicide, and then finally she gets to that sub-human state and he determines to imprison her at Thornfield under the surveillance of Grace Poole. Bertha is cunning, working out her escapes when Grace Poole is slightly the worse for drink. She abstracts the key to the room and, obsessed with a hatred of those close to her, and even seeming to understand what is going on with regard to the marriage, attacks both Rochester and her brother Richard. It is almost as if she blames them for her incarceration, trying to burn Rochester in his bed and biting her brother so badly that a surgeon has to dress his wounds. Yet she spares Jane on the eve of the wedding, despite the ripping up of the veil. Fire continues to be her chief resource of destruction, and she sets fire to the bed in which Jane would have been sleeping at Thornfield. She dies, but she has something of a terrible revenge in the mutilation of Rochester. She jumps to her death in the courtyard below, a scene perhaps indebted to Ulrica's leap in Scott's *Ivanhoe*, one of Charlotte's favourite novels.

Richard Mason

With his quivering limbs and white cheeks.

Richard Mason is a weak character who apparently cannot keep away from his sister; tormented himself by the madness inherent in the family and its prospective manifestation in him, he comes to see her at Thornfield and reaps the whirlwind of her savagery. He recovers after treatment but later, when he has learned that Rochester intends to commit bigamy by marrying Jane, he employs his lawyer to stop the marriage ceremony. Here he displays cowardice, since he could have gone to Rochester himself, and it is noticeable that the lawyer has to urge him to keep up his courage once the attempted bigamy is disclosed. Rochester is obviously contemptuous of him – he reveals that Mason once displayed a 'dog-like' devotion to him – and when Mason cowers he observes 'Cheer up, Dick – never fear me! – I'd almost as soon strike a woman as you.' His role in the action is functional, and in view of what the future holds for him, pathetic.

Diana and Mary Rivers

Two young, graceful women – ladies in every point.

St John's sisters are attractive, intelligent, infinitely likeable characters though, like Jane, we should probably prefer Diana. When Jane first sees them they are studying German; some time later, when Jane has recovered, Diana offers to give her lessons in that language, and she proves to be a good teacher. She is vivacious and energetic, obviously the leader of the two, and she is also warm and sympathetic. She secretly hopes that Jane will marry St John, but knows her brother well and understands Jane's natural rejection of him. Although 'She looked and spoke with a certain authority' and 'she had a will, evidently' she has none of the coldness of her autocratic brother; in fact she is flexible and giving. In Diana Charlotte's characterization is seen to advantage, for although she is good she is not cloying. Mary, the younger sister, is pretty, intelligent but has more the distance and reserve of her brother, though as she gets to know Jane she is affectionate towards her. Note how both sisters accept Jane's share of her inheritance without any false pride or protestation, just as they stoically accepted earlier that the fortune they had expected to come their way was – ironically – for someone else – that someone else later proving to be Jane. Both sisters are delighted that they are able to give up their posts as governesses and return home.

Rosamond Oliver

She was hasty, but good-humoured . . . every glance in the glass showed her a flush of loveliness . . . but she was not profoundly interesting or thoroughly impressive . . .

This is a minor character, but in relation to St John she has an important functional role. She is very beautiful, but because

St John has virtually denied the flesh he denies her. Rosamond puts herself in his company as much as possible, tries to get him to go home and visit her father with her, visits the school where Jane is and where St John often is, but all to no avail. One can see that physically she complements St John, but that is all. Had he remained a clergyman it is just conceivable that she would have been an acceptable wife for him, but St John is clear-sighted enough to recognize that as a missionary's wife she would be completely out of her sphere and, more accurately, out of his too. St John's face 'flushed and kindled' when he first looked at her in Jane's presence, but it is significant that when she is about to be married to Mr Granby, St John, in giving the news, is as 'serene as glass'. Rosamond is coquettish but not heartless, she has been indulged all her life by her wealthy and adoring father, but she is not objectionable or selfish, though I think it could be asserted that she is shallow. She certainly knows the power of her beauty, knows also St John loves her, but can make nothing of the fact that his response to her is so inhibited. Jane fittingly compares Rosamond to Adèle Varens – 'gay, lively, unthinking and charming'.

Structure and style

Structure

Jane Eyre is an account of the heroine's journey through life from childhood up to her marriage with Rochester, with a look into the future some ten years on. The first part is Jane in adversity at Gateshead, bullied, lied about and finally despatched to Lowood after her fearful interview with the un-Christian Mr Brocklehurst. The second part traces her career at Lowood, initially in adversity again, but making friends with Helen Burns, loving her and Miss Temple, and gradually being allowed to develop her love of learning, showing that she has both discipline and ability. This takes us up to Jane deciding to leave Lowood after the departure of Miss Temple, now married; although the narrative viewpoint is consistent, eight years are passed over in a sentence or so. With her arrival at Thornfield Jane enters on the third phase of her life; she demonstrates her capacity to be useful in a number of ways, firstly to Adèle, then casually and socially to Mrs Fairfax, and thirdly practically and romantically to Rochester. She is also able to indulge her bent for observation, a marked character trait, and we note her keenness when Blanche Ingram and the rest of the house-guests are under her eye.

The fourth phase sees Jane's return to Gateshead to see the dying Mrs Reed, whose conscience has been troubling her over her treatment of Jane; it should be noted that this comes at a crisis point in Jane's life, since she is expecting that Rochester will marry Blanche Ingram. Jane's decision to see Mrs Reed emphasizes her moral responsibility. That her devotion to duty brings its own reward is seen here in the revelation that her uncle in Madeira has written to Mrs Reed and, though he believes on that lady's authority that Jane is dead, it sets in train that section of the plot which ultimately leads to Jane's inheritance and her division of it with her cousins. The fifth section of the novel marks Jane's return to Thornfield, her acceptance of Rochester's marriage proposal, Jane's seeing the mad woman in her room, the broken-off marriage ceremony and the meeting with Rochester's mad wife. It ends with Jane leaving Thornfield, and the sixth section deals with Jane's flight, her arrival at Moor House, her inheritance and her relationship with her cousins, the proposal from St John Rivers that she should accompany him to India and, the pivotal point of the novel, Jane's hearing Rochester's voice. The seventh phase is the rest of the story – Jane's return to a ruined Thornfield, her discovery of a physically ruined Rochester, her marriage to him, the look into their married life, the news of St John Rivers' impending death. The command of narrative tension throughout each of these sections is what gives *Jane Eyre* its main appeal. As I have observed earlier, and it needs to be repeated, the binding adhesive of *Jane Eyre* is the consistency of the narrative viewpoint. Each section flows into the next with the natural sequence of events.

Style

Charlotte Brontë's style in *Jane Eyre* is quite distinctive. Take the opening of the novel:

There was no possibility of taking a walk that day. We had been wandering, indeed, in the leafless shrubbery an hour in the morning . . . the cold winter wind had brought with it clouds so sombre, and a rain so penetrating . . .

Note that this vitally establishes the *mood* of the opening chapters while Jane is in adversity. It is plain, straightforward writing but also has a symbolic overtone, that is to say the mood here fits the mood of the writing in terms of character. This is one of Charlotte Brontë's favourite devices, and she uses it to telling and explicit effect later in the novel when, as Jane and Rochester are in the garden, there comes a storm:

And what ailed the chestnut tree? it writhed and groaned; while wind roared in the laurel-walk and came sweeping over us.

They go in, but the next morning Adèle comes to Jane with the news:

that the great horse-chestnut tree at the bottom of the orchard had been struck by lightning in the night, and half of it split away.

Now, the storm occasioned by Rochester's attempted marriage with Jane is still to break; when it does we see Rochester as a split man, divided between the imprisoned mad wife and the possibility of living with Jane. But that is not all; Rochester is stricken by the injuries he receives in the fire. When he talks to Jane of his state he observes 'I am no better than the lightning-struck chestnut-tree in Thornfield orchard' as if all the time he has been aware of his own association with it. Here the symbol is used as forecast, but it is also used within character to show a kind of pathetic awareness of connection.

The use of the symbolic association is very strong in *Jane Eyre*, since the figurative language enhances our appreciation of Jane's situation – she is compared to a trapped bird on a number of occasions, the irony being that she is trapped but does not know it by the fact that Rochester's wife is living. But if we leave aside the metaphorical mode, we are left with a superb simplicity and directness, perhaps seen at its best in the dialogue. When Rochester and Jane converse, when she parries his impetuosity, or when St John Rivers undertakes his spiritual blackmail of Jane, we are aware that the style is the speaker, that Charlotte is able to characterize very strongly because it is not merely the physical trait but the linguistic trait she is concentrating on. Thus Rochester seeks to reassure Jane just before the wedding:

Now, Janet, I'll explain to you all about it. It was half-dream, half-reality: a woman did, I doubt not, enter your room: and that woman was – must have been – Grace Poole.

Note that the half-sentences are half thoughts on the way to an explanation, the index to the working of Rochester's mind, a mind at once quick, impetuous, conscious of his own deception. Here by way of contrast is St John Rivers:

... it is not me you deny, but God. Through my means, He opens to you a noble career; as my wife only can you enter upon it. Refuse to be my wife, and you limit yourself for ever to a track of selfish ease and barren obscurity.

Note here the careful choice of words with their attendant irony; St John calls Jane selfish, but it is he who is selfish. He uses the word 'barren' which is not definitive of Jane but is certainly definitive of St John's own approach to her.

Charlotte Brontë is the mistress of the word-picture, whether it be of an individual or of a scene. *Jane Eyre* is as vivid and immediate as the pictures that Jane herself paints (these almost certainly have symbolic associations in the text). Take the contrast betweeen Blanche Ingram and the beautiful Rosamond

Oliver; both are set compellingly before the reader, the 'strapper' and the heiress who cannot understand why St John Rivers spurns her virtually proffered love. Take the scene where Rochester conducts Jane and those present at the 'wedding' ceremony to see the bestial creature who pads before them; this is Charlotte Brontë depicting people and situation with a terrifying realism. This realism, despite the incidence of the romantic and the Gothic, runs throughout *Jane Eyre*, from the little child's understandable fears in the red room, through being set on a stool before everybody at Lowood, through watching her veil rent by the creature in her room, through to her carrying the tray in to the near-blind Rochester and making herself lovingly known to him. Since the narrative of Jane runs the whole length of the novel, we had better add that she is depicted, as are Rochester and St John Rivers, and even the minor characters like, for example, Eliza Reed, with psychological consistency, the major strand of realism in characterization.

There is, too, the natural realism of scene, as when Jane is in Hay Lane, where she first meets Rochester, and where she describes the natural seasonal changes of 'wild roses in summer, for nuts and blackberries in autumn, and even now possessing a few coral treasures in hips and haws, but whose best winter delight lay in its utter solitude and leafless repose'. This is outdoor visual and associative, like the love scene in the garden at midsummer, but interiors are just as tellingly described, like the red room, the schoolroom at Lowood and, best of all, the room into which Jane looks from the outside when she first sees Diana and Mary working.

Throughout *Jane Eyre* the author shows a keen sense of the dramatic, as we have seen from the description of the horse-chestnut tree. 'Grace Poole's' laugh is redolent of drama, Jane's first meeting with Rochester and the latter's sudden revelation of himself as the gipsy, plus Rochester enlisting Jane's aid in the middle of the night to sit with the wounded Richard Mason, all these are dramatic, and indeed *Jane Eyre* has many dramatic moments. Sometimes these are catalogued in the natural terms which Jane so often employs, as when with her 'marriage' ruined she observes 'A Christmas frost had come at Midsummer; a white December storm had whirled over June ... I came into deep waters; the floods overflowed me.' And with this last phrase there is almost a biblical echo. References to the Bible are many and various in *Jane Eyre*, and they are a subtle way of underlining Jane's own Christianity and faith, her determination throughout to live and act by moral principles. At the same time we note the naturalness of Adèle's French, how the language itself somehow conveys the sophistication to which Adèle herself would aspire. It must be admitted that there are instances, fortunately precious few, where some of Jane's statements are pedantic, dated, and show a conscious straining after literary effects, here antithesis: 'The human and the fallible should not arrogate a power with which the divine and perfect alone can be safely entrusted.'

The use of the first person narrator in the novel has both advantages and disadvantages. The major advantage is the reader's identification with the character, a kind of intimacy which is assisted by the style, since Jane (Charlotte) addresses the reader, confides, points out, explains. The chief disadvantage is that the central character often does not know what is happening – for example, with the mystery over Grace Poole, or even the gipsy disguise used by Rochester which Jane, amazingly, does not penetrate. But these in a way act positively as well, since they contribute to narrative tension. Moreover, as mentioned earlier, the narrative viewpoint is consistent. Jane's tone may vary according to circumstances, but we are aware of her throughout as a positive and consistent person. Thus when the marriage falls through, we know, because we have come to know Jane so well, that she will not stay at Thornfield. We know, though Jane does not fully grasp this, that in seeing St John as beautiful she is also seeing in her consciousness the man who is not beautiful but whom she loves. So consistent is Charlotte Brontë in her presentation of Jane that we are almost inclined to equate the fictional character with her creator. It would be dangerous to do so, except that on one level, the level of romance, the novel exists as a kind of wish-fulfilment – 'Reader, I married him.' Yet the style of *Jane Eyre* is so admirably direct, so true to life, so free from dressing or vacuous ornamentation, that it keeps our attention and furthers our excitement. It is high narrative art.

General questions and questions on related topics for coursework/examinations or other books you may be studying

1 In what ways is Charlotte Brontë a dramatic writer? Answer with reference to *Jane Eyre*.

Suggested notes for essay answer:

(a) Define 'dramatic' – immediacy of appeal – moving/exciting/frightening qualities, etc. – use of expectation/suspense/ fear/the unusual/ supernatural, etc.

(b) Dramatic qualities of *Jane Eyre* – pathos/fear in red room incident (or Jane's attack on John Reed) – Jane's meeting with Brocklehurst – the latter's visit to Lowood – Jane's punishment – death of Helen Burns.

(c) At Thornfield: Grace Poole's laugh – meeting with Rochester – the fire in Rochester's room – Rochester as gipsy – the attack on Mason.

(d) The wedding and its aftermath.

(e) At Moor House: St John's proposal – Rochester's voice.

(f) Jane's finding the ruin of Thornfield – the ruin that is Rochester – the drama of his blindness, etc.

(g) Conclusion – list under categories given in (a) the main dramatic qualities in *Jane Eyre* and the author's successful employment of dramatic device.

2 In what ways do you regard Charlotte Brontë as a shrewd and observant writer in *Jane Eyre*? Quote and refer in support of your views.

3 What do you learn from this novel of the treatment of governesses in the nineteenth century?

4 What do you learn about the position of women in the first half of the nineteenth century from *Jane Eyre*?

5 Thackeray considered that the plot of *Jane Eyre* was hackneyed. How far do you agree with his judgement?

6 'With less skilful treatment *Jane Eyre* might have become a melodrama.' Say how far you agree or disagree with this statement.

7 Write an essay on Charlotte Brontë's ability to maintain suspense in *Jane Eyre*.

8 In what ways do you find Jane herself imaginative? Refer closely to the text in your answer.

9 'She is a cloying little prig.' Write an essay in defence of Jane, bearing this statement in mind.

10 Write an essay on Charlotte Brontë's use of (a) contrast and (b) coincidence in *Jane Eyre*.

11 Write a detailed account of one episode which you find *either* (a) pathetic *or* (b) humorous.

12 In what ways is Charlotte Brontë a realistic novelist? You should refer closely to the text in your answer.

13 In what ways does Charlotte Brontë succeed in creating an atmosphere of mystery in *Jane Eyre*?

14 Write a detailed account of the character of Rochester.

15 Write an essay on the part played in the plot by (a) Adèle (b) Helen Burns.

16 Write an account of the part played in the plot by (a) Mr Mason and (b) Grace Poole.

17 Write an account of the most important aspects of the house-party which Mr Rochester gives at Thornfield.

18 Write a detailed study of the character of St John Rivers.

19 Compare and contrast Diana and Mary Rivers with Rosamond Oliver.

20 Discuss Charlotte Brontë's use of either natural description or of symbolism in *Jane Eyre*.

21 In what ways is Jane a godfearing Christian?

22 Compare and contrast Mrs Fairfax and Mrs Reed.

23 Compare and contrast Georgiana and Eliza Reed.

24 Show how Charlotte Brontë builds up an atmosphere of fear in any two episodes.

25 Write an essay on any aspect of *Jane Eyre* not covered by the questions above.

26 Write about any book you have read in which the story is told autobiographically.

27 Give an account of any *two* journeys and their consequences in any book you are studying.

28 Using material in your chosen book, write about school life as it affected the leading character or characters.

29 Explain clearly how one of the characters in your book is faced with a difficult decision and how he or she resolves it.

30 Write about an unusual or mysterious happening in one of the books you are studying.

31 Give an account of a strong or dominating personality in a novel or story of your choice.

Further reading

Other novels by Charlotte Brontë:

Shirley
Villette

Novels by Emily and Anne Brontë:
Wuthering Heights
The Tenant of Wildfell Hall

Biography:
The Life of Charlotte Brontë, Mrs E. Gaskell (Dent).
Charlotte Brontë: The Evolution of Genius, Winifred Gérin (OUP).

Critical appreciation:
Everyman's Companion to the Brontës, Barbara and Gareth
Lloyd Evans (Dent).